D0641286

THREE CENTURIES OF
ENGLISH ESSAYS

THREE CENTURIES OF
ENGLISH ESSAYS

From FRANCIS BACON *to*
MAX BEERBOHM

EDITED BY
V. H. COLLINS

Essay Index Reprint Series

BOOKS FOR LIBRARIES PRESS
FREEPORT, NEW YORK

First Published 1931
Reprinted 1967

STANDARD BOOK NUMBER:
8369-0327-7

LIBRARY OF CONGRESS CATALOG CARD NUMBER:
67-26727

PRINTED IN THE UNITED STATES OF AMERICA

CONTENTS

INTRODUCTION

For the earliest source of the Essay one must go back to the ancients. Aristotle, in his *Ethics*, portrayed the characteristics of the ideal man who constituted a mean between various extreme vices. Theophrastus (died 287 B.C.) followed up this method in his *Characters*. These consist of studies of different types of men—the Garrulous Man, the Back-Biter, the Flatterer, the Grumbler, the Bore, &c. They have had a numerous progeny through the ages, and they influenced the novel, though later developments of this have been away from the type, towards the complex individual.

The first essayist proper was Montaigne (1533–93), who, moreover, was the first to call this form of writing 'essay'. The French, however, as well as the Germans—who have borrowed the term 'essayist'—have tended to regard the essay as indigenous to England, and to ascribe its perfection to the line of English essayists which began with Bacon. In some ways Bacon imitated Montaigne. In other ways he is much less like Montaigne than are the most famous of those who succeeded him: 'the Lord Chancellor writes in his robe of office; Montaigne in his *robe de chambre*'. Montaigne is like an informal, charming friend. In Bacon's hands the essay is very often not much more than a string of maxims. There is neither tenderness nor humour; there are no shadows and no colour: the only illumination is the dry light of reason.

The first examples in our language of that intimate tone which is a characteristic of the true essay are to be found in the essays of Abraham Cowley (1618–67). Unlike Bacon, Cowley wrote with no didactic aim, but with tenderness, pity, and personal reminiscence.

Meanwhile the 'Character' pieces of certain writers in the seventeenth century—John Earle (1601–65), Francis Quarles (1592–1644), and others—following the model of Theophrastus, had introduced into English literature a type of composition which was to exercise influence on the next stage of the essay. The articles written for the *Tatler* and *Spectator* by Addison and Steele showed a new feature in the incisive sketch of character, as seen in the creation of the immortal Sir Roger de Coverley. The members of the Spectator Club began as stock characters—the Squire, the Templar, the Man about Town, &c.—but Addison fell in love with the Squire, bagged him from Steele, and developed him into a real, live, individual character (the essay thus pointing on to the novel).

The direction given to the essay by Addison and Steele was followed in the middle of the eighteenth century by Goldsmith. As an essayist Goldsmith comes off best in the *Chinese Letters* (afterwards reprinted as the *Citizen of the World*). The chief feature of the most lively of these papers was again characterization. Johnson, in his multitudinous papers in the *Rambler* and *Idler*, was less happy—his heavy and pompous tread being ill-suited to obtain that effect of unstudied ease which is required by the short treatment of a light theme.

Towards the end of the eighteenth century the essay reached what still to-day seems to be its final form. Four writers stand out at this stage: de Quincey, Leigh Hunt, Hazlitt, and Lamb. De Quincey, with his rhetoric and elaborate machinery, belongs to a class of his own. In the other three the essay takes on its distinctive qualities—intimate; conversational; genial; witty. It breaks away, for good, from that professorial attitude and moralizing spirit—an inheritance from its philosophical origin—which to our modern taste makes many of the papers in the *Tatler* and *Spectator* insufferably boring, and which allowed Johnson, even when treating such a light topic as the use of our hours of ease, to warn us that 'our amusements should not terminate wholly in the present moment, but should contribute more or less to future advantage', and that one should amuse oneself among well-chosen companions in order that 'the loose sparkles of thoughtless wit may give new light to the mind, and the gay contention for paradoxical positions rectify the opinions'.

As compared with the difference between Addison and Lamb, any development which has taken place since the latter has been negligible. The best essays of to-day retain the characteristics which Lamb perfected, and to which can be applied a description he himself gives in an essay on the owners of 'Imperfect Sympathies'—'They have no pretences to much clearness or precision in their ideas, or in their manner of expressing them. Their intellectual wardrobe has few whole pieces in it. They are content with fragments and scattered pieces of truth. The light that lights them is not steady and polar, but mutable and shifting; waxing and again waning.'

FRANCIS BACON

OF FRIENDSHIP

It had been hard for him that spake it to have put more truth and untruth together in few words than in that speech, *Whosoever is delighted in solitude, is either a wild beast or a god*: for it is most true, that a natural and secret hatred and aversation towards society in any man hath somewhat of the savage beast; but it is most untrue that it should have any character at all of the divine nature, except it proceed, not out of a pleasure in solitude, but out of a love and desire to sequester a man's self for a higher conversation: such as is found to have been falsely and feignedly in some of the heathen; as Epimenides, the Candian; Numa, the Roman; Empedocles, the Sicilian; and Apollonius of Tyana; and truly and really in divers of the ancient hermits and holy fathers of the Church. But little do men perceive what solitude is, and how far it extendeth; for a crowd is not company, and faces are but a gallery of pictures, and talk but a tinkling cymbal, where there is no love. The Latin adage meeteth with it a little, *Magna civitas, magna solitudo*; because in a great town friends are scattered, so that there is not that fellowship, for the most part, which is in less neighbourhoods. But we may go further, and affirm most truly, that it is a mere and miserable solitude to want true friends, without which the world is but a wilderness; and even in this sense also of solitude, whosoever in the frame of his nature and affections is unfit for friendship, he taketh it of the beast, and not from humanity.

A principal fruit of friendship is the ease and discharge of the fulness and swellings of the heart, which passions of all kinds do cause and induce. We know diseases of stoppings and suffocations are the most dangerous in the body; and it is not much otherwise in the mind; you may take sarza to open the liver, steel to open the spleen, flowers of sulphur for the lungs, castoreum for the brain;

but no receipt openeth the heart but a true friend, to whom you may impart griefs, joys, fears, hopes, suspicions, counsels, and whatsoever lieth upon the heart to oppress it, in a kind of civil shrift or confession.

It is a strange thing to observe how high a rate great kings and monarchs do set upon this fruit of friendship whereof we speak: so great, as they purchase it many times at the hazard of their own safety and greatness: for princes, in regard of the distance of their fortune from that of their subjects and servants, cannot gather this fruit, except (to make themselves capable thereof) they raise some persons to be as it were companions, and almost equals to themselves, which many times sorteth to inconvenience. The modern languages give unto such persons the name of favourites or privadoes, as if it were matter of grace or conversation; but the Roman name attaineth the true use and cause thereof, naming them *participes curarum*: for it is that which tieth the knot. And we see plainly that this hath been done, not by weak and passionate princes only, but by the wisest and most politic that ever reigned, who have oftentimes joined to themselves some of their servants, whom both themselves have called friends, and allowed others likewise to call them in the same manner, using the word which is received between private men.

L. Sylla, when he commanded Rome, raised Pompey (after surnamed the Great) to that height that Pompey vaunted himself for Sylla's overmatch; for when he had carried the consulship for a friend of his, against the pursuit of Sylla, and that Sylla did a little resent thereat, and began to speak great, Pompey turned upon him again, and in effect bade him be quiet; *for that more men adored the sun rising than the sun setting*. With Julius Caesar, Decimus Brutus had obtained that interest, as he set him down in his testament for heir in remainder after his nephew; and this was the man that had power with him to draw him forth to his death: for when Caesar would have discharged the senate, in regard of some ill presages and specially a dream of Calpurnia, this man

lifted him gently by the arm out of his chair, telling him
he hoped he would not dismiss the senate till his wife had
dreamt a better dream ; and it seemeth his favour was so
great, as Antonius, in a letter which is recited verbatim
in one of Cicero's Philippics, calleth him *venefica*—'witch' ;
as if he had enchanted Caesar. Augustus raised Agrippa
(though of mean birth) to that height, as, when he con-
sulted with Maecenas about the marriage of his daughter
Julia, Maecenas took the liberty to tell him, *that he must
either marry his daughter to Agrippa, or take away his life:
there was no third way, he had made him so great.* With
Tiberius Caesar, Sejanus had ascended to that height as
they two were termed and reckoned as a pair of friends.
Tiberius, in a letter to him, saith, *Haec pro amicitia
nostra non occultavi*; and the whole senate dedicated an
altar to Friendship, as to a goddess, in respect of the
great dearness of friendship between them two. The like,
or more, was between Septimius Severus and Plautianus ;
for he forced his eldest son to marry the daughter of
Plautianus, and would often maintain Plautianus in
doing affronts to his son ; and did write also in a letter to
the senate by these words: *I love the man so well as I wish
he may over-live me.* Now, if these princes had been as a
Trajan, or a Marcus Aurelius, a man might have thought
that this had proceeded of an abundant goodness of
nature ; but being men so wise, of such strength and
severity of mind, and so extreme lovers of themselves,
as all these were, it proveth most plainly that they found
their own felicity (though as great as ever happened to
mortal men) but as an half-piece, except they might have a
friend to make it entire ; and yet, which is more, they were
princes that had wives, sons, nephews ; and yet all these
could not supply the comfort of friendship.

It is not to be forgotten what Comineus observeth of
his first master, Duke Charles the Hardy ; namely, that
he would communicate his secrets with none ; and least of
all those secrets which troubled him most. Whereupon
he goeth on and saith that towards his latter time *that
closeness did impair and a little perish his understanding.*

Surely Comineus might have made the same judgement also, if it had pleased him, of his second master, Louis the Eleventh, whose closeness was indeed his tormentor. The parable of Pythagoras is dark but true, *Cor ne edito*—'*Eat not the heart*'. Certainly, if a man would give it a hard phrase, those that want friends to open themselves unto are cannibals of their own hearts. But one thing is most admirable (wherewith I will conclude this first fruit of friendship), which is, that this communicating of a man's self to his friend works two contrary effects; for it redoubleth joys, and cutteth griefs in halves: for there is no man that imparteth his joys to his friend, but he joyeth the more; and no man that imparteth his griefs to his friend, but he grieveth the less. So that it is, in truth of operation upon a man's mind, of like virtue as the alchemists used to attribute to their stone for man's body, that it worketh all contrary effects, but still to the good and benefit of nature: but yet, without praying in aid of alchemists, there is a manifest image of this in the ordinary course of nature; for, in bodies, union strengtheneth and cherisheth any natural action, and, on the other side, weakeneth and dulleth any violent impression; and even so is it of minds.

The second fruit of friendship is healthful and sovereign for the understanding, as the first is for the affections; for friendship maketh indeed a fair day in the affections from storm and tempests, but it maketh daylight in the understanding, out of darkness and confusion of thoughts: neither is this to be understood only of faithful counsel, which a man receiveth from his friend; but before you come to that, certain it is that whosoever hath his mind fraught with many thoughts, his wits and understanding do clarify and break up in the communicating and discoursing with another; he tosseth his thoughts more easily; he marshalleth them more orderly; he seeth how they look when they are turned into words: finally, he waxeth wiser than himself; and that more by an hour's discourse than by a day's meditation. It was well said by Themistocles to the king of Persia, *That speech was like cloth of*

*Arras opened and put abroad; whereby the imagery doth
appear in figure; whereas in thoughts they lie but as in packs.*
Neither is this second fruit of friendship, in opening the
understanding, restrained only to such friends as are able
to give a man counsel (they indeed are best); but even
without that a man learneth of himself, and bringeth his
own thoughts to light, and whetteth his wits as against a
stone which itself cuts not. In a word, a man were better
relate himself to a statua or picture, than to suffer his
thoughts to pass in smother.

Add now, to make this second fruit of friendship complete, that other point which lieth more open, and falleth
within vulgar observation: which is faithful counsel from
a friend. Heraclitus saith well in one of his enigmas, *Dry
light is ever the best*: and certain it is that the light that
a man receiveth by counsel from another is drier and
purer than that which cometh from his own understanding and judgement; which is ever infused and drenched
in his affections and customs. So there is as much difference between the counsel that a friend giveth, and that a
man giveth himself, as there is between the counsel of a
friend and of a flatterer; for there is no such flatterer as is a
man's self, and there is no such remedy against flattery of
a man's self as the liberty of a friend. Counsel is of two
sorts; the one concerning manners, the other concerning
business. For the first, the best preservative to keep the
mind in health is the faithful admonition of a friend. The
calling of a man's self to a strict account is a medicine
sometimes too piercing and corrosive; reading good books
of morality is a little flat and dead; observing our faults
in others is sometimes unproper for our case; but the best
receipt (best, I say, to work and best to take) is the
admonition of a friend. It is a strange thing to behold
what gross errors and extreme absurdities many (especially of the greater sort) do commit for want of a friend to
tell them of them, to the great damage both of their fame
and fortune: for, as St. James saith, they are as men *that
look sometimes into a glass, and presently forget their own
shape and favour.* As for business, a man may think, if he

will, that two eyes see no more than one; or that a game-
ster seeth always more than a looker-on; or that a man in
anger is as wise as he that hath said over the four and
twenty letters; or that a musket may be shot off as well
upon the arm as upon a rest; and such other fond and
high imaginations, to think himself all in all. But when
all is done, the help of good counsel is that which setteth
business straight: and if any man think that he will take
counsel, but it shall be by pieces, asking counsel in one
business of one man, and in another business of another
man, it is well (that is to say, better perhaps than if he
asked none at all); but he runneth two dangers; one, that
he shall not be faithfully counselled; for it is a rare thing,
except it be from a perfect and entire friend, to have counsel
given but such as shall be bowed and crooked to some
ends which he hath that giveth it: the other, that he shall
have counsel given hurtful and unsafe (though with good
meaning), and mixed partly of mischief and partly of
remedy; even as if you would call a physician, that is
thought good for the cure of the disease you complain of,
but is unacquainted with your body; and therefore may
put you in a way for a present cure, but overthroweth
your health in some other kind, and so cure the disease
and kill the patient: but a friend that is wholly acquainted
with a man's estate will beware, by furthering any present
business, how he dasheth upon other inconvenience; and
therefore rest not upon scattered counsels; they will
rather distract and mislead than settle and direct.

After these two noble fruits of friendship (peace in the
affections, and support of the judgement), followeth the
last fruit, which is like the pomegranate, full of many
kernels; I mean aid, and bearing a part in all actions and
occasions. Here the best way to represent to life the
manifold use of friendship is to cast and see how many
things there are which a man cannot do himself; and then
it will appear that it was a sparing speech of the ancients
to say, *that a friend is another himself*: for that a friend is
far more than himself. Men have their time, and die
many times in desire of some things which they principally

take to heart; the bestowing of a child, the finishing of a work, or the like. If a man have a true friend, he may rest almost secure that the care of those things will continue after him; so that a man hath, as it were, two lives in his desires. A man hath a body, and that body is confined to a place: but where friendship is, all offices of life are as it were granted to him and his deputy; for he may exercise them by his friend. How many things are there which a man cannot, with any face or comeliness, say or do himself? A man can scarce allege his own merits with modesty, much less extol them: a man cannot sometimes brook to supplicate or beg, and a number of the like: but all these things are graceful in a friend's mouth, which are blushing in a man's own. So again, a man's person hath many proper relations which he cannot put off. A man cannot speak to his son but as a father; to his wife but as a husband; to his enemy but upon terms: whereas a friend may speak as the case requires, and not as it sorteth with the person. But to enumerate these things were endless; I have given the rule where a man cannot fitly play his own part; if he have not a friend, he may quit the stage.

JOSEPH ADDISON

SIR ROGER AT CHURCH

'Αθανάτους μὲν πρῶτα θεούς, νόμῳ ὡς διάκειται,
Τίμα——   PYTHAGORAS.

I AM always very well pleased with a country Sunday,
and think, if keeping holy the seventh day were only
a human institution, it would be the best method that
could have been thought of for the polishing and civilizing
of mankind. It is certain the country people would soon
degenerate into a kind of savages and barbarians were
there not such frequent returns of a stated time in which
the whole village meet together with their best faces, and
in their cleanliest habits, to converse with one another
upon indifferent subjects, hear their duties explained to
them, and join together in adoration of the Supreme
Being. Sunday clears away the rust of the whole week,
not only as it refreshes in their minds the notions of
religion, but as it puts both the sexes upon appearing in
their most agreeable forms, and exerting all such qualities
as are apt to give them a figure in the eye of the village.
A country fellow distinguishes himself as much in the
churchyard as a citizen does upon the Change, the whole
parish politics being generally discussed in that place
either after sermon or before the bell rings.

My friend Sir Roger, being a good churchman, has
beautified the inside of his church with several texts of
his own choosing; he has likewise given a handsome
pulpit-cloth, and railed in the communion table at his
own expense. He has often told me, that at his coming
to his estate he found his parishioners very irregular;
and that in order to make them kneel and join in the
responses he gave every one of them a hassock and a
common-prayer book: and at the same time employed an
itinerant singing master, who goes about the country for
that purpose, to instruct them rightly in the tunes of the
psalms; upon which they now very much value them-

selves, and indeed outdo most of the country churches that I have ever heard.

As Sir Roger is landlord to the whole congregation, he keeps them in very good order, and will suffer nobody to sleep in it besides himself; for if by chance he has been surprised into a short nap at sermon, upon recovering out of it he stands up and looks about him, and if he sees anybody else nodding, either wakes them himself, or sends his servants to them. Several other of the old knight's particularities break out upon these occasions: sometimes he will be lengthening out a verse in the singing-psalms, half a minute after the rest of the congregation have done with it; sometimes, when he is pleased with the matter of his devotion, he pronounces *Amen* three or four times to the same prayer; and sometimes stands up when everybody else is upon their knees, to count the congregation, or see if any of his tenants are missing.

I was yesterday very much surprised to hear my old friend, in the midst of the service, calling out to one John Matthews to mind what he was about, and not disturb the congregation. This John Matthews it seems is remarkable for being an idle fellow, and at that time was kicking his heels for his diversion. This authority of the knight, though exerted in that odd manner which accompanies him in all circumstances of life, has a very good effect upon the parish, who are not polite enough to see anything ridiculous in his behaviour; besides that the general good sense and worthiness of his character makes his friends observe these little singularities as foils that rather set off than blemish his good qualities.

As soon as the sermon is finished, nobody presumes to stir till Sir Roger is gone out of the church. The knight walks down from his seat in the chancel between a double row of his tenants, that stand bowing to him on each side; and every now and then inquires how such an one's wife, or mother, or son, or father do, whom he does not see at church; which is understood as a secret reprimand to the person that is absent.

The chaplain has often told me, that upon a catechising day, when Sir Roger has been pleased with a boy that answers well, he has ordered a bible to be given him next day for his encouragement; and sometimes accompanies it with a flitch of bacon to his mother. Sir Roger has likewise added five pounds a year to the clerk's place; and that he may encourage the young fellows to make themselves perfect in the church service, has promised, upon the death of the present incumbent, who is very old, to bestow it according to merit.

The fair understanding between Sir Roger and his chaplain, and their mutual concurrence in doing good, is the more remarkable, because the very next village is famous for the differences and contentions that rise between the parson and the squire, who live in a perpetual state of war. The parson is always preaching at the squire, and the squire to be revenged on the parson never comes to church. The squire has made all his tenants atheists, and tithe-stealers; while the parson instructs them every Sunday in the dignity of his order, and insinuates to them in almost every sermon that he is a better man than his patron. In short, matters are come to such an extremity, that the squire has not said his prayers either in public or private this half year; and that the parson threatens him, if he does not mend his manners, to pray for him in the face of the whole congregation.

Feuds of this nature, though too frequent in the country, are very fatal to the ordinary people; who are so used to be dazzled with riches, that they pay as much deference to the understanding of a man of an estate, as of a man of learning: and are very hardly brought to regard any truth, how important soever it may be, that is preached to them, when they know there are several men of five hundred a year who do not believe it.

MEDITATIONS IN WESTMINSTER ABBEY

Pallida mors æquo pulsat pede pauperum tabernas
Regumque turres. O beate Sesti,
Vitæ summa brevis spem nos vetat inchoare longam.
Iam te premet nox, fabulæque manes,
Et domus exilis Plutonia.   Hor.

WHEN I am in a serious humour, I very often walk by
myself in Westminster Abbey, where the gloominess of
the place, and the use to which it is applied, with the
solemnity of the building, and the condition of the people
who lie in it, are apt to fill the mind with a kind of
melancholy, or rather thoughtfulness, that is not disagreeable. I yesterday passed a whole afternoon in the
churchyard, the cloisters, and the church, amusing myself with the tombstones and inscriptions that I met with
in those several regions of the dead. Most of them recorded nothing else of the buried person, but that he was
born upon one day, and died upon another; the whole
history of his life being comprehended in those two circumstances that are common to all mankind. I could
not but look upon these registers of existence, whether
of brass or marble, as a kind of satire upon the departed
persons; who had left no other memorial of them, but
that they were born and that they died. They put me
in mind of several persons mentioned in the battles of
heroic poems, who have sounding names given them, for
no other reason but that they may be killed, and are
celebrated for nothing but being knocked on the head.

Γλαῦκόν τε Μέδοντά τε Θερσίλοχόν τε. Hom.
Glaucumque, Medontaque, Thersilochumque. Virg.

The life of these men is finely described in holy writ by
'the path of an arrow,' which is immediately closed up
and lost.
 Upon my going into the church I entertained myself
with the digging of a grave; and saw in every shovelful
of it that was thrown up, the fragment of a bone or skull

B 2

intermixed with a kind of fresh mouldering earth, that some time or other had a place in the composition of a human body. Upon this I began to consider with myself what innumerable multitudes of people lay confused together under the pavement of that ancient cathedral; how men and women, friends and enemies, priests and soldiers, monks and prebendaries, were crumbled amongst one another, and blended together in the same common mass; how beauty, strength, and youth, with old age, weakness, and deformity, lay undistinguished in the same promiscuous heap of matter.

After having thus surveyed this great magazine of mortality, as it were, in the lump, I examined it more particularly by the accounts which I found on several of the monuments which are raised in every quarter of that ancient fabric. Some of them were covered with such extravagant epitaphs, that, if it were possible for the dead person to be acquainted with them, he would blush at the praises which his friends have bestowed upon him. There are others so excessively modest, that they deliver the character of the person departed in Greek or Hebrew, and by that means are not understood once in a twelve-month. In the poetical quarter I found there were poets who had no monuments, and monuments which had no poets. I observed, indeed, that the present war had filled the church with many of these uninhabited monuments, which had been erected to the memory of persons whose bodies were perhaps buried in the plains of Blenheim, or in the bosom of the ocean.

I could not but be very much delighted with several modern epitaphs which are written with great elegance of expression and justness of thought, and therefore do honour to the living as well as to the dead. As a foreigner is very apt to conceive an idea of the ignorance or polite-ness of a nation from the turn of their public monuments and inscriptions, they should be submitted to the perusal of men of learning and genius, before they are put in execution. Sir Cloudesley Shovel's monument has very often given me great offence: instead of the brave rough

English Admiral, which was the distinguishing character of that plain gallant man, he is represented on his tomb by the figure of a beau, dressed in a long periwig, and reposing himself upon velvet cushions under a canopy of state. The inscription is answerable to the monument; for instead of celebrating the many remarkable actions he had performed in the service of his country, it acquaints us only with the manner of his death, in which it was impossible for him to reap any honour. The Dutch, whom we are apt to despise for want of genius, show an infinitely greater taste of antiquity and politeness in their buildings and works of this nature, than what we meet with in those of our own country. The monuments of their admirals, which have been erected at the public expense, represent them like themselves; and are adorned with rostral crowns and naval ornaments, with beautiful festoons of seaweed, shells, and coral.

But to return to our subject. I have left the repository of our English kings for the contemplation of another day, when I shall find my mind disposed for so serious an amusement. I know that entertainments of this nature are apt to raise dark and dismal thoughts in timorous minds and gloomy imaginations; but for my own part, though I am always serious, I do not know what it is to be melancholy; and can therefore take a view of nature in her deep and solemn scenes, with the same pleasure as in her most gay and delightful ones. By this means I can improve myself with those objects which others consider with terror. When I look upon the tombs of the great, every emotion of envy dies in me; when I read the epitaphs of the beautiful, every inordinate desire goes out; when I meet with the grief of parents upon a tombstone, my heart melts with compassion; when I see the tomb of the parents themselves, I consider the vanity of grieving for those whom we must quickly follow; when I see kings lying by those who deposed them, when I consider rival wits placed side by side, or the holy men that divided the world with their contests and disputes, I reflect with sorrow and astonishment on the little competitions,

factions, and debates of mankind. When I read the several
dates of the tombs, of some that died yesterday, and
some six hundred years ago, I consider that great day
when we shall all of us be contemporaries, and make our
appearance together.

OLIVER GOLDSMITH

BEAU TIBBS, A CHARACTER

THOUGH naturally pensive, yet I am fond of gay company, and take every opportunity of thus dismissing the mind from duty. From this motive I am often found in the centre of a crowd; and wherever pleasure is to be sold, am always a purchaser. In those places, without being remarked by any, I join in whatever goes forward, work my passions into a similitude of frivolous earnestness, shout as they shout, and condemn as they happen to disapprove. A mind thus sunk for a while below its natural standard is qualified for stronger flights; as those first retire who would spring forward with greater vigour.

Attracted by the serenity of the evening, a friend and I lately went to gaze upon the company in one of the public walks near the city. Here we sauntered together for some time, either praising the beauty of such as were handsome, or the dresses of such as had nothing else to recommend them. We had gone thus deliberately forward for some time, when my friend stopping on a sudden caught me by the elbow, and led me out of the public walk; I could perceive, by the quickness of his pace, and by his frequently looking behind, that he was attempting to avoid somebody who followed; we now turned to the right, then to the left; as we went forward, he still went faster, but in vain; the person whom he attempted to escape hunted us through every doubling, and gained upon us each moment; so that, at last, we fairly stood still, resolving to face what we could not avoid.

Our pursuer soon came up, and joined us with all the familiarity of an old acquaintance. 'My dear Charles,' cries he, shaking my friend's hand, 'where have you been hiding this half a century? Positively I had fancied you were gone down to cultivate matrimony and your estate in the country.' During the reply I had an opportunity of surveying the appearance of our new companion. His

hat was pinched up with peculiar smartness; his looks
were pale, thin, and sharp; round his neck he wore a
broad black ribbon, and in his bosom a buckle studded
with glass; his coat was trimmed with tarnished twist;
he wore by his side a sword with a black hilt; and his
stockings of silk, though newly washed, were grown
yellow by long service. I was so much engaged with the
peculiarity of his dress, that I attended only to the latter
part of my friend's reply, in which he complimented
Mr. Tibbs on the taste of his clothes, and the bloom in
his countenance. 'Psha, psha, Charles,' cried the figure,
'no more of that if you love me; you know I hate flattery,
on my soul I do; and yet to be sure an intimacy with the
great will improve one's appearance, and a course of
venison will fatten; and yet, faith, I despise the great as
much as you do; but there are a great many damned
honest fellows among them; and we must not quarrel
with one half because the other wants breeding. If they
were all such as my Lord Mudler, one of the most good-
natured creatures that ever squeezed a lemon, I should
myself be among the number of their admirers. I was
yesterday to dine at the Duchess of Piccadilly's. My lord
was there. "Ned," says he to me, "Ned," says he, "I'll
hold gold to silver I can tell where you were poaching
last night." "Poaching, my lord," says I; "faith, you
have missed already; for I stayed at home and let the
girls poach for me." That's my way; I take a fine woman
as some animals do their prey; stand still, and swoop,
they fall into my mouth.'

'Ah, Tibbs, thou art a happy fellow,' cried my companion with looks of infinite pity, 'I hope your fortune
is as much improved as your understanding in such
company?' 'Improved!' replied the other; 'you shall
know—but let it go no farther—a great secret—five
hundred a year to begin with—my lord's word of honour
for it—his lordship took me down in his own chariot
yesterday, and we had a tête-à-tête dinner in the country,
where we talked of nothing else.' 'I fancy you forgot,
sir, cried I, 'you told us but this moment of your dining

yesterday in town!' 'Did I say so?' replied he coolly.
'To be sure, if I said so it was so. Dined in town: egad,
now I do remember I did dine in town; but I dined in
the country too: for you must know, my boys, I eat two
dinners. By the by, I am grown as nice as the devil in
my eating. I'll tell you a pleasant affair about that: we
were a select party of us to dine at Lady Grogram's: an
affected piece, but let it go no farther; a secret. Well,
says I, I'll hold a thousand guineas, and say done first,
that—but, dear Charles, you are an honest creature, lend
me half-a-crown for a minute or two, or so, just till—but
hark'e, ask me for it the next time we meet, or it may
be twenty to one but I forget to pay you.'

When he left us, our conversation naturally turned
upon so extraordinary a character. 'His very dress,' cries
my friend, 'is not less extraordinary than his conduct.
If you meet him this day, you find him in rags; if the
next, in embroidery. With those persons of distinction,
of whom he talks so familiarly, he has scarce a coffee-
house acquaintance. However, both for the interest of
society, and perhaps for his own, Heaven has made him
poor; and, while all the world perceives his wants, he
fancies them concealed from every eye. An agreeable
companion, because he understands flattery; and all must
be pleased with the first part of his conversation, though
all are sure of its ending with a demand on their purse.
While his youth countenances the levity of his conduct,
he may thus earn a precarious subsistence; but, when
age comes on, the gravity of which is incompatible with
buffoonery, then will he find himself forsaken by all—
condemned in the decline of life to hang upon some rich
family whom he once despised, there to undergo all the
ingenuity of studied contempt; to be employed only as
a spy upon the servants, or a bugbear to fright children
into duty.'

TO THE PRINTER

Sir,

I am the same Common Council-man who troubled you some days ago. To whom can I complain but to you? for you have many a dismal correspondent; in this time of joy my wife does not choose to hear me, because she says I'm always melancholy when she's in spirits. I have been to see the Coronation, and a fine sight it was, as I am told. To those who had the pleasure of being near spectators, the diamonds, I am told, were as thick as Bristol stones in a show-glass; the ladies and gentlemen walked all along, one foot before another, and threw their eyes about them, on this side and that, perfectly like clock-work. Oh! Mr. Printer, it had been a fine sight indeed, if there was but a little more eating.

Instead of that, there we sat, penned up in our scaffoldings, like sheep upon a market-day in Smithfield; but the devil a thing could I get to eat (God pardon me for swearing) except the fragments of a plum-cake, that was all squeezed into crumbs in my wife's pocket, as she came through the crowd.

You must know, sir, that in order to do the thing genteelly, and that all my family might be amused at the same time, my wife, my daughter, and I, took two guinea places for the Coronation, and I gave my two eldest boys (who, by the by, are twins, fine children) eighteenpence apiece to go to Sudrick Fair, to see the court of the Black King of Morocco, which will serve to please children well enough.

That we might have good places on the scaffolding, my wife insisted upon going at seven o'clock the evening before the Coronation, for she said she would not lose a full prospect for the world. This resolution I own shocked me. 'Grizzle,' said I to her, 'Grizzle, my dear, consider that you are but weakly, always ailing, and will never bear sitting out all night upon the scaffold. You remember what a cold you caught the last fast-day, by rising but half an hour before your time to go to church,

and how I was scolded as the cause of it. Beside, my
dear, our daughter Anna Amelia Wilhelmina Carolina
will look like a perfect fright, if she sits up, and you
know the girl's face is something at her time of life, considering her fortune is but small.' 'Mr. Grogan,' replied
my wife, 'Mr. Grogan, this is always the case, when you
find me in spirits; I don't want to go, not I; nor I don't
care whether I go at all; it is seldom that I am in spirits;
but this is always the case.' In short, Mr. Printer, what
will you have on't?—to the Coronation we went.

What difficulties we had in getting a coach, how we
were shoved about in the mob, how I had my pocket
picked of the last new almanac, and my steel tobacco-
box; how my daughter lost half an eyebrow and her laced
shoe in a gutter; my wife's lamentation upon this, with
the adventures of the crumbled plum cake, and broken
brandy-bottle, what need I relate all these? We suffered
this and ten times more before we got to our places.

At last, however, we were seated. My wife is certainly
a heart of oak; I thought sitting up in the damp night
air would have killed her; I have known her for two
months take possession of our easy-chair, mobbed up in
flannel nightcaps, and trembling at a breath of air; but
she now bore the night as merrily as if she had sat up
at a christening. My daughter and she did not seem to
value it of a farthing. She told me two or three stories
that she knows will always make me laugh, and my
daughter sung me the 'Noontide Air,' towards one o'clock
in the morning. However, with all their endeavours I was
as cold and as dismal as ever I remember. If this be the
pleasures of a coronation, cried I to myself, I had rather
see the court of King Solomon in all his glory at my ease
in Bartholomew Fair.

Towards morning sleep began to come fast upon me;
and the sun rising and warming the air still inclined me
to rest a little. You must know, sir, that I am naturally
of a sleepy constitution; I have often sat up at table
with my eyes open, and have been asleep all the while.
What will you have on't? Just about eight o'clock in the

morning I fell fast asleep. I fell into the most pleasing dream in the world. I shall never forget it; I dreamed that I was at my Lord Mayor's feast, and had scaled the crust of a venison pasty. I kept eating and eating, in my sleep, and thought I could never have enough. After some time the pasty methought was taken away, and the dessert was brought in its room. Thought I to myself, if I have not got enough of the venison, I am resolved to make it up by the largest snap at the sweetmeats. Accordingly I grasped a whole pyramid; the rest of the guests seeing me with so much, one gave me a snap, and the other gave me a snap, I was pulled this way by my neighbour on the right hand, and that by my neighbour on the left, but still kept my ground without flinching, and continued eating and pocketing as fast as I could. I never was so pulled and hauled in my whole life. At length, however, going to smell to a lobster that lay before me, methought it caught me with its claws fast by the nose. The pain I felt upon this occasion is inexpressible; in fact it broke my dream; when, awaking, I found my wife and daughter applying a smelling-bottle to my nose; and telling me it was time to go home, they assured me every means had been tried to awake me, while the procession was going forward, but that I still continued to sleep till the whole ceremony was over. Mr. Printer, this is a hard case, and as I read your most ingenious work, it will be some comfort, when I see this inserted, to find that——I write for it too.

I am, Sir,

Your distressed, humble servant,
L. GROGAN.

CHARLES LAMB

CHRIST'S HOSPITAL FIVE-AND-THIRTY YEARS AGO

In Mr. Lamb's *Works*, published a year or two since, I find a magnificent eulogy on my old school, such as it was, or now appears to him to have been, between the years 1782 and 1789. It happens, very oddly, that my own standing at Christ's was nearly corresponding with his; and, with all gratitude to him for his enthusiasm for the cloisters, I think he has contrived to bring together whatever can be said in praise of them, dropping all the other side of the argument most ingeniously.

I remember L. at school; and can well recollect that he had some peculiar advantages, which I and others of his schoolfellows had not. His friends lived in town, and were near at hand; and he had the privilege of going to see them, almost as often as he wished, through some invidious distinction, which was denied to us. The present worthy sub-treasurer to the Inner Temple can explain how that happened. He had his tea and hot rolls in a morning, while we were battening upon our quarter of a penny loaf—our *crug*—moistened with attenuated small beer, in wooden piggins, smacking of the pitched leathern jack it was poured from. Our Monday's milk porridge, blue and tasteless, and the pease soup of Saturday, coarse and choking, were enriched for him with a slice of 'extraordinary bread and butter', from the hot-loaf of the Temple. The Wednesday's mess of millet, somewhat less repugnant (we had three banyan to four meat days in the week)—was endeared to his palate with a lump of double-refined, and a smack of ginger (to make it go down the more glibly) or the fragrant cinnamon. In lieu of our *half-pickled* Sundays, or *quite fresh* boiled beef on Thursdays (strong as *caro equina*), with detestable marigolds floating in the pail to poison the broth—our scanty mutton scrags on Fridays—and rather more savoury, but

grudging, portions of the same flesh, rotten-roasted or
rare, on the Tuesdays (the only dish which excited our
appetites, and disappointed our stomachs, in almost equal
proportion)—he had his hot plate of roast veal, or the
more tempting griskin (exotics unknown to our palates),
cooked in the paternal kitchen (a great thing), and
brought him daily by his maid or aunt! I remember the
good old relative (in whom love forbade pride) squatting
down upon some odd stone in a by-nook of the cloisters,
disclosing the viands (of higher regale than those cates
which the ravens ministered to the Tishbite); and the
contending passions of L. at the unfolding. There was
love for the bringer; shame for the thing brought, and
the manner of its bringing; sympathy for those who were
too many to share in it; and, at top of all, hunger (eldest,
strongest of the passions!) predominant, breaking down
the stony fences of shame, and awkwardness, and a
troubling overconsciousness.

I was a poor friendless boy. My parents, and those
who should care for me, were far away. Those few
acquaintances of theirs, whom they could reckon upon
as being kind to me in the great city, after a little forced
notice, which they had the grace to take of me on my
first arrival in town, soon grew tired of my holiday visits.
They seemed to them to recur too often, though I thought
them few enough; and, one after another, they all failed
me, and I felt myself alone among six hundred playmates.

O the cruelty of separating a poor lad from his early
homestead! The yearnings which I used to have towards
it in those unfledged years! How, in my dreams, would
my native town (far in the west) come back, with its
church, and trees, and faces! How I would wake weeping,
and in the anguish of my heart exclaim upon sweet Calne
in Wiltshire!

To this late hour of my life, I trace impressions left by
the recollection of those friendless holidays. The long
warm days of summer never return but they bring with
them a gloom from the haunting memory of those *whole-
day leaves*, when, by some strange arrangement, we were

turned out, for the live-long day, upon our own hands, whether we had friends to go to, or none. I remember those bathing-excursions to the New River, which L. recalls with such relish, better, I think, than he can—for he was a home-seeking lad, and did not much care for such water-pastimes. How merrily we would sally forth into the fields; and strip under the first warmth of the sun; and wanton like young dace in the streams; getting us appetites for noon, which those of us that were penniless (our scanty morning crust long since exhausted) had not the means of allaying—while the cattle, and the birds, and the fishes, were at feed about us, and we had nothing to satisfy our cravings—the very beauty of the day, and the exercise of the pastime, and the sense of liberty, setting a keener edge upon them! How faint and languid, finally, we would return, towards nightfall, to our desired morsel, half-rejoicing, half-reluctant, that the hours of our uneasy liberty had expired!

It was worse in the days of winter, to go prowling about the streets objectless—shivering at cold windows of print shops, to extract a little amusement; or haply, as a last resort, in the hopes of a little novelty, to pay a fifty-times repeated visit (where our individual faces should be as well known to the warden as those of his own charges) to the Lions in the Tower—to whose levée, by courtesy immemorial, we had a prescriptive title to admission.

L.'s governor (so we called the patron who presented us to the foundation) lived in a manner under his paternal roof. Any complaint which he had to make was sure of being attended to. This was understood at Christ's, and was an effectual screen to him against the severity of masters, or worse tyranny of the monitors. The oppressions of these young brutes are heart-sickening to call to recollection. I have been called out of my bed, and *waked for the purpose,* in the coldest winter nights—and this not once, but night after night—in my shirt, to receive the discipline of a leathern thong, with eleven other sufferers, because it pleased my callow overseer, when there has

been any talking heard after we were gone to bed, to
make the six last beds in the dormitory, where the
youngest children of us slept, answerable for all offence
they neither dared to commit, nor had the power to
hinder. The same execrable tyranny drove the younger
part of us from the fires, when our feet were perishing
with snow; and, under the cruellest penalties, forbade the
indulgence of a drink of water, when we lay in sleepless
summer nights, fevered with the season and the day's
sports.

There was one H——, who, I learned in after days,
was seen expiating some maturer offence in the hulks.
(Do I flatter myself in fancying that this might be the
planter of that name, who suffered –at Nevis, I think,
or St. Kitts—some few years since? My friend Tobin
was the benevolent instrument of bringing him to the
gallows.) This petty Nero actually branded a boy, who
had offended him, with a red-hot iron; and nearly starved
forty of us, with exacting contributions, to the one-half
of our bread, to pamper a young ass, which, incredible as
it may seem, with the connivance of the nurse's daughter
(a young flame of his) he had contrived to smuggle in,
and keep upon the leads of the *ward*, as they called our
dormitories. This game went on for better than a week,
till the foolish beast, not able to fare well but he must
cry roast meat—happier than Caligula's minion, could he
have kept his own counsel—but, foolisher, alas! than any
of his species in the fables—waxing fat, and kicking, in
the fullness of bread, one unlucky minute would needs
proclaim his good fortune to the world below; and, laying
out his simple throat, blew such a ram's horn blast, as
(toppling down the walls of his own Jericho) set conceal-
ment any longer at defiance. The client was dismissed,
with certain attentions, to Smithfield; but I never understood that the patron underwent any censure on the
occasion. This was in the stewardship of L.'s admired
Perry.

Under the same *facile* administration, can L. have
forgotten the cool impunity with which the nurses used

to carry away openly, in open platters, for their own
tables, one out of two of every hot joint, which the careful
matron had been seeing scrupulously weighed out for our
dinners? These things were daily practised in that magnificent apartment, which L. (grown connoisseur since,
we presume) praises so highly for the grand paintings
'by Verrio and others', with which it is 'hung round and
adorned'. But the sight of sleek well-fed blue-coat boys
in pictures was, at that time, I believe, little consolatory
to him, or us, the living ones, who saw the better part of
our provisions carried away before our faces by harpies;
and ourselves reduced (with the Trojan in the hall of
Dido)

> To feed our mind with idle portraiture.

L. has recorded the repugnance of the school to *gags*, or
the fat of fresh beef boiled; and sets it down to some
superstition. But these unctuous morsels are never grate-
ful to young palates (children are universally fat-haters),
and in strong, coarse, boiled meats, *unsalted*, are detestable. A *gag-eater* in our time was equivalent to a ghoul,
and held in equal detestation. —— suffered under the
imputation:

> ... 'Twas said
> He ate strange flesh.

He was observed, after dinner, carefully to gather up
the remnants left at his table (not many, nor very choice
fragments, you may credit me)—and, in an especial
manner, these disreputable morsels, which he would con-
vey away, and secretly stow in the settle that stood at his
bedside. None saw when he ate them. It was rumoured
that he privately devoured them in the night. He was
watched, but no traces of such midnight practices were
discoverable. Some reported, that, on leave-days, he had
been seen to carry out of the bounds a large blue check
handkerchief, full of something. This then must be the
accursed thing. Conjecture next was at work to imagine
how he could dispose of it. Some said he sold it to the
beggars. This belief generally prevailed. He went about

moping. None spake to him. No one would play with him. He was excommunicated; put out of the pale of the school. He was too powerful a boy to be beaten, but he underwent every mode of that negative punishment which is more grievous than many stripes. Still he persevered. At length he was observed by two of his school-fellows, who were determined to get at the secret, and had traced him one leave-day for that purpose, to enter a large worn-out building, such as there exist specimens of in Chancery Lane, which are let out to various scales of pauperism, with open door, and a common staircase. After him they silently slunk in, and followed by stealth up four flights, and saw him tap at a poor wicket, which was opened by an aged woman, meanly clad. Suspicion was now ripened into certainty. The informers had secured their victim. They had him in their toils. Accusation was formally preferred, and retribution most signal was looked for. Mr. Hathaway, the then steward (for this happened a little after my time), with that patient sagacity which tempered all his conduct determined to investigate the matter, before he proceeded to sentence. The result was that the supposed mendicants, the receivers or purchasers of the mysterious scraps, turned out to be the parents of ——, an honest couple come to decay—whom this seasonable supply had, in all probability, saved from mendicancy: and that this young stork, at the expense of his own good name, had all this while been only feeding the old birds! The governors on this occasion, much to their honour, voted a present relief to the family of ——, and presented him with a silver medal. The lesson which the steward read upon RASH JUDGEMENT, on the occasion of publicly delivering the medal to ——, I believe, would not be lost upon his auditory. I had left school then, but I well remember ——. He was a tall, shambling youth, with a cast in his eye, not at all calculated to conciliate hostile prejudices. I have since seen him carrying a baker's basket. I think I heard he did not do quite so well by himself as he had done by the old folks.

I was a hypochondriac lad; and the sight of a boy in
fetters, upon the day of my first putting on the blue
clothes, was not exactly fitted to assuage the natural
terrors of initiation. I was of tender years, barely turned
of seven; and had only read of such things in books, or
seen them but in dreams. I was told he had *run away*.
This was the punishment for the first offence. As a novice
I was soon after taken to see the dungeons. These were
little, square, Bedlam cells, where a boy could just lie
at his length upon straw and a blanket—a mattress, I
think, was afterwards substituted—with a peep of light,
let in askance, from a prison-orifice at top, barely enough
to read by. Here the poor boy was locked in by himself all
day, without sight of any but the porter who brought him
his bread and water—who *might not speak to him*—or of
the beadle, who came twice a week to call him out to
receive his periodical chastisement, which was almost wel-
come, because it separated him for a brief interval from
solitude—and here he was shut up by himself *of nights*,
out of the reach of any sound, to suffer whatever horrors
the weak nerves, and superstition incident to his time of
life, might subject him to.[1] This was the penalty for the
second offence. Wouldst thou like, Reader, to see what
became of him in the next degree?

The culprit, who had been a third time an offender, and
whose expulsion was at this time deemed irreversible, was
brought forth, as at some solemn *auto-da-fé*, arrayed in
uncouth and most appalling attire; all trace of his late
'watchet-weeds' carefully effaced, he was exposed in a
jacket, resembling those which London lamplighters
formerly delighted in, with a cap of the same. The effect
of this divestiture was such as the ingenious devisers of it
could have anticipated. With his pale and frightened
features, it was as if some of those disfigurements in

[1] One or two instances of lunacy, or attempted suicide, accordingly, at length convinced the governors of the impolicy of this part
of the sentence, and the midnight torture to the spirits was dispensed
with. This fancy of dungeons for children was a sprout of Howard's
brain; for which (saving the reverence due to Holy Paul) methinks
I could willingly spit upon his statue.

Dante had seized upon him. In this disguisement he was brought into the hall (*L.'s favourite state-room*), where awaited him the whole number of his schoolfellows, whose joint lessons and sports he was thenceforth to share no more; and the awful presence of the steward, to be seen for the last time; of the executioner beadle, clad in his state robe for the occasion; and of two faces more, of direr import, because never but in these extremities visible. These were governors; two of whom, by choice, or charter, were always accustomed to officiate at these *ultima supplicia*—not to mitigate (so at least we understood it), but to enforce the uttermost stripe. Old Bamber Gascoigne, and Peter Aubert, I remember, were colleagues on one occasion, when, the beadle turning rather pale, a glass of brandy was ordered to prepare him for the mysteries. The scourging was, after the old Roman fashion, long and stately. The lictor accompanied the criminal quite round the hall. We were generally too faint with attending to the previous disgusting circumstances to make accurate report with our eyes of the degree of corporal suffering inflicted. Report, of course, gave out the back knotty and livid. After scourging, he was made over, in his san benito, to his friends, if he had any (but commonly such poor runagates were friendless), or to his parish officer, who, to enhance the effect of the scene, had his station allotted to him on the outside of the hall gate.

These solemn pageantries were not played off so often as to spoil the general mirth of the community. We had plenty of exercise and recreation *after* school hours; and, for myself, I must confess that I was never happier than *in* them. The Upper and the Lower Grammar Schools were held in the same room; and an imaginary line only divided their bounds. Their character was as different as that of the inhabitants on the two sides of the Pyrenees. The Rev. James Boyer was the Upper Master, but the Rev. Matthew Field presided over that portion of the apartment of which I had the good fortune to be a member. We lived a life as careless as birds. We talked and did just what we pleased, and nobody molested us. We carried an Accidence, or a Grammar, for form; but, for any trouble it gave us, we might take two years in getting through the verbs deponent, and another two in forgetting all that we had learned about them. There was now and then the formality of saying a lesson, but if you had not learned it, a brush across the shoulders (just enough to disturb a fly) was the sole remonstrance. Field never used the rod; and in truth he wielded the cane with no great goodwill--holding it 'like a dancer'. It looked in his hands rather like an emblem than an instrument of authority; and an emblem, too, he was ashamed of. He was a good easy man, that did not care to ruffle his own peace, nor perhaps set any great consideration upon the value of juvenile time. He came among us, now and then, but often stayed away whole days from us; and when he came, it made no difference to us—he had his private room to retire to, the short time he stayed, to be out of the sound of our noise. Our mirth and uproar went on. We had classics of our own, without being beholden to 'insolent Greece or haughty Rome', that passed current among us—*Peter Wilkins*—*The Adventures of the Hon. Captain Robert Boyle*—*The Fortunate Blue-coat Boy*—and the like. Or we cultivated a turn for mechanic and scientific operations; making little sun-dials of paper; or weaving those ingenious parentheses called *cat-cradles*; or making dry peas to dance upon the end of a tin pipe; or studying the art military over that laudable game 'French and English', and a hundred other such devices to pass away the time—mixing the useful with the agreeable—as would have made the souls of Rousseau and John Locke chuckle to have seen us.

Matthew Field belonged to that class of modest divines who affect to mix in equal proportion the *gentleman*, the *scholar*, and the *Christian*; but, I know not how, the first ingredient is generally found to be the predominating dose in the composition. He was engaged in gay parties, or with his courtly bow at some episcopal levée, when he should have been attending upon us. He had for many years the classical charge of a hundred children, during the four or five first years of their education; and his very highest form seldom proceeded further than two or three of the introductory fables of Phaedrus. How things were suffered to go on thus, I cannot guess. Boyer, who was the proper person to have remedied these abuses, always affected, perhaps felt, a delicacy in interfering in a province not strictly his own. I have not been without my suspicions that he was not altogether displeased at the contrast we presented to his end of the school. We were a sort of Helots to his young Spartans. He would sometimes, with ironic deference, send to borrow a rod of the Under Master, and then, with sardonic grin, observe to one of his upper boys, 'how neat and fresh the twigs looked.' While his pale students were battering their brains over Xenophon and Plato, with a silence as deep as that enjoined by the Samite, we were enjoying ourselves at our ease in our little Goshen. We saw a little into the secrets of his discipline, and the prospect did but the more reconcile us to our lot. His thunders rolled innocuous for us; his storms came near, but never touched us; contrary to Gideon's miracle, while all around were drenched, our fleece was dry. His boys turned out the better scholars; we, I suspect, have the advantage in temper. His pupils cannot speak of him without something of terror allaying their gratitude; the remembrance of Field comes back with all the soothing images of indolence, and summer slumbers, and work like play, and innocent idleness, and Elysian exemptions, and life itself a 'playing holiday'.

Though sufficiently removed from the jurisdiction of Boyer, we were near enough (as I have said) to understand a little of his system. We occasionally heard sounds of the *Ululantes*, and caught glances of Tartarus. B. was a rabid pedant. His English style was cramped to barbarism. His Easter anthems (for his duty obliged him to those periodical flights) were grating as scrannel pipes.[1]

[1] In this and everything B. was the antipodes of his coadjutor. While the former was digging his brains for crude anthems, worth

He would laugh—ay, and heartily—but then it must be
at Flaccus's quibble about *Rex*—— or at the *tristis
severitas in vultu,* or *inspicere in patinas,* of Terence—
thin jests, which at their first broaching could hardly have
had *vis* enough to move a Roman muscle. He had two
wigs, both pedantic, but of different omen: the one serene,
smiling, fresh powdered, betokening a mild day; the other,
an old discoloured, unkempt, angry caxon, denoting frequent and bloody execution. Woe to the school, when he
made his morning appearance in his *passy,* or *passionate
wig.* No comet expounded surer. J. B. had a heavy hand.
I have known him double his knotty fist at a poor trembling child (the maternal milk hardly dry upon its lips)
with a 'Sirrah, do you presume to set your wits at me?'
Nothing was more common than to see him make a headlong entry into the schoolroom, from his inner recess, or
library, and, with turbulent eye, singling out a lad, roar
out, 'Od's my life, sirrah' (his favourite adjuration), 'I
have a great mind to whip you'—then, with as sudden a
retracting impulse, fling back into his lair—and, after a
cooling lapse of some minutes (during which all but the
culprit had totally forgotten the context) drive headlong
out again, piecing out his imperfect sense, as if it had been
some Devil's Litany, with the expletory yell—'*and I
will too.*' In his gentler moods, when the *rabidus furor*
was assuaged, he had resort to an ingenious method,
peculiar, for what I have heard, to himself, of whipping
the boy, and reading the Debates, at the same time; a
paragraph and a lash between; which in those times,
when parliamentary oratory was most at a height and
flourishing in these realms, was not calculated to impress
the patient with a veneration for the diffuser graces of
rhetoric.

a pig-nut, F. would be recreating his gentlemanly fancy in the more
flowery walks of the Muses. A little dramatic effusion of his, under
the name of *Vertumnus and Pomona,* is not yet forgotten by the
chroniclers of that sort of literature. It was accepted by Garrick,
but the town did not give it their sanction. B. used to say of it, in
a way of half-compliment, half-irony, that it was *too classical for
representation.*

Once, and but once, the uplifted rod was known to fall ineffectual from his hand—when droll squinting W—— having been caught putting the inside of the master's desk to a use for which the architect had clearly not designed it, to justify himself, with great simplicity averred, that *he did not know that the thing had been fore-warned.* This exquisite irrecognition of any law ante-cedent to the *oral* or *declaratory* struck so irresistibly upon the fancy of all who heard it (the pedagogue him-self not excepted) that remission was unavoidable.

L. has given credit to B.'s great merits as an instructor. Coleridge, in his literary life, has pronounced a more intelligible and ample encomium on them. The author of the *Country Spectator* doubts not to compare him with the ablest teachers of antiquity. Perhaps we cannot dismiss him better than with the pious ejaculation of C. when he heard that his old master was on his death-bed: 'Poor J. B.! may all his faults be forgiven; and may he be wafted to bliss by little cherub boys, all head and wings, with no *bottoms* to reproach his sublunary infirmi-ties.'

Under him were many good and sound scholars bred. First Grecian of my time was Lancelot Pepys Stevens, kindest of boys and men, since Co-grammar-master (and inseparable companion) with Dr. T——e. What an edify-ing spectacle did this brace of friends present to those who remembered the anti-socialities of their predecessors! You never met the one by chance in the street without a wonder, which was quickly dissipated by the almost immediate sub-appearance of the other. Generally arm-in-arm, these kindly coadjutors lightened for each other the toilsome duties of their profession, and when, in advanced age, one found it convenient to retire, the other was not long in discovering that it suited him to lay down the fasces also. Oh, it is pleasant, as it is rare, to find the same arm linked in yours at forty, which at thirteen helped it to turn over Cicero *De Amicitia*, or some tale of Antique Friendship, which the young heart even then **was** burning to anticipate! Co-Grecian with S. was

Th——, who has since executed with ability various
diplomatic functions at the Northern courts. Th——
was a tall, dark, saturnine youth, sparing of speech, with
raven locks. Thomas Fanshaw Middleton followed him
(now Bishop of Calcutta), a scholar and a gentleman in
his teens. He has the reputation of an excellent critic;
and is author (besides the *Country Spectator*) of a treatise
on the Greek Article, against Sharpe. M. is said to bear
his mitre high in India, where the *regni novitas* (I dare say)
sufficiently justifies the bearing. A humility quite as
primitive as that of Jewel or Hooker might not be exactly
fitted to impress the minds of those Anglo-Asiatic dio-
cesans with a reverence for home institutions, and the
church which those fathers watered. The manners of M.
at school, though firm, were mild and unassuming. Next
to M. (if not senior to him) was Richards, author of *The
Aboriginal Britons*, the most spirited of the Oxford Prize
Poems; a pale, studious Grecian. Then followed poor
S——, ill-fated M——! Of these the Muse is silent.

> Finding some of Edward's race
> Unhappy, pass their annals by.

Come back into memory, like as thou wert in the day-
spring of thy fancies, with hope like a fiery column before
thee—the dark pillar not yet turned—Samuel Taylor
Coleridge—Logician, Metaphysician, Bard! How have I
seen the casual passer through the Cloisters stand still,
entranced with admiration (while he weighed the dispro-
portion between the *speech* and the *garb* of the young
Mirandola) to hear thee unfold, in thy deep and sweet
intonations, the mysteries of Iamblichus, or Plotinus (for
even in those years thou waxedst not pale at such philosophic draughts), or reciting Homer in his Greek, or
Pindar—— while the walls of the old Grey Friars re-
echoed to the accents of the *inspired charity-boy*! Many
were the 'wit-combats' (to dally awhile with the words of
old Fuller), between him and C. V. Le G——, 'which two
I behold like a Spanish great galleon, and an English man-
of-war. Master Coleridge, like the former, was built far

higher in learning, solid, but slow in his performances. Le G., with the English man-of-war, lesser in bulk, but lighter in sailing, could turn with all times, tack about, and take advantage of all winds, by the quickness of his wit and invention'.

Nor shalt thou, their compeer, be quickly forgotten, Allen, with the cordial smile, and still more cordial laugh, with which thou wert wont to make the old Cloisters shake, in thy cognition of some poignant jest of theirs; or the anticipation of some more material, and peradventure practical one, of thine own. Extinct are those smiles, with that beautiful countenance, with which (for thou wert the *Nireus formosus* of the school), in the days of thy maturer waggery, thou didst disarm the wrath of infuriated town-damsel, who, incensed by provoking pinch, turning tigress-like round, suddenly converted by thy angel-look, exchanged the half-formed terrible '*bl*——', for a gentler greeting—'*bless thy handsome face!*'

Next follow two, who ought to be now alive, and the friends of Elia—the junior Le G—— and F——; who impelled, the former by a roving temper, the latter by too quick a sense of neglect—ill capable of enduring the slights poor Sizars are sometimes subject to in our seats of learning—exchanged their Alma Mater for the camp; perishing, one by climate, and one on the plains of Salamanca: Le G——, sanguine, volatile, sweet-natured; F——, dogged, faithful, anticipative of insult, warm-hearted, with something of the old Roman height about him.

Fine, frank-hearted Fr——, the present master of Hertford, with Marmaduke T——, mildest of Missionaries —and both my good friends still—close the catalogue of Grecians in my time.

THE CONVALESCENT

A PRETTY severe fit of indisposition which, under the name of a nervous fever, has made a prisoner of me for some weeks past, and is but slowly leaving me, has reduced me to an incapacity of reflecting upon any topic foreign to itself. Expect no healthy conclusions from me this month, reader; I can offer you only sick men's dreams.

And truly the whole state of sickness is such; for what else is it but a magnificent dream for a man to lie a-bed, and draw day-light curtains about him; and, shutting out the sun, to induce a total oblivion of all the works which are going on under it? To become insensible to all the operations of life, except the beatings of one feeble pulse?

If there be a regal solitude, it is a sick bed. How the patient lords it there! What caprices he acts without control! How king-like he sways his pillow—tumbling, and tossing, and shifting, and lowering, and thumping, and flatting, and moulding it, to the ever varying requisitions of his throbbing temples.

He changes *sides* oftener than a politician. Now he lies full length, then half-length, obliquely, transversely, head and feet quite across the bed; and none accuses him of tergiversation. Within the four curtains he is absolute. They are his Mare Clausum.

How sickness enlarges the dimensions of a man's self to himself! He is his own exclusive object. Supreme selfishness is inculcated upon him as his only duty. 'Tis the Two Tables of the Law to him. He has nothing to think of but how to get well. What passes out of doors, or within them, so he hear not the jarring of them, affects him not.

A little while ago he was greatly concerned in the event of a law-suit, which was to be the making or the marring of his dearest friend. He was to be seen trudging about upon this man's errand to fifty quarters of the town at once, jogging this witness, refreshing that solicitor. The cause was to come on yesterday. He is absolutely as

indifferent to the decision as if it were a question to be
tried at Pekin. Peradventure from some whispering,
going on about the house, not intended for his hearing,
he picks up enough to make him understand that things
went cross-grained in the Court yesterday, and his friend
is ruined. But the word 'friend', and the word 'ruin,'
disturb him no more than so much jargon. He is not to
think of anything but how to get better.

What a world of foreign cares are merged in that absorb-
ing consideration!

He has put on the strong armour of sickness, he is
wrapped in the callous hide of suffering; he keeps his
sympathy, like some curious vintage, under trusty lock
and key, for his own use only.

He lies pitying himself, honing and moaning to himself; he yearneth over himself; his bowels are even melted
within him, to think what he suffers; he is not ashamed
to weep over himself.

He is for ever plotting how to do some good to himself;
studying little stratagems and artificial alleviations.

He makes the most of himself; dividing himself, by an
allowable fiction, into as many distinct individuals as he
hath sore and sorrowing members. Sometimes he medi-
tates—as of a thing apart from him—upon his poor
aching head, and that dull pain which, dozing or waking,
lay in it all the past night like a log, or palpable substance
of pain, not to be removed without opening the very skull,
as it seemed, to take it thence. Or he pities his long,
clammy, attenuated fingers. He compassionates himself
all over; and his bed is a very discipline of humanity and
tender heart.

He is his own sympathizer; and instinctively feels that
none can so well perform that office for him. He cares for
few spectators to his tragedy. Only that punctual face of
the old nurse pleases him, that announces his broths, and
his cordials. He likes it because it is so unmoved, and
because he can pour forth his feverish ejaculations before
it as unreservedly as to his bed-post.

To the world's business he is dead. He understands not

what the callings and occupations of mortals are ; only he
has a glimmering conceit of some such thing, when the
doctor makes his daily call: and even in the lines of that
busy face he reads no multiplicity of patients, but solely
conceives of himself as *the sick man.* To what other uneasy
couch the good man is hastening, when he slips out of his
chamber, folding up his thin douceur so carefully for fear
of rustling, 'is no speculation which he can at present
entertain. He thinks only of the regular return of the
same phenomenon at the same hour to-morrow.

Household rumours touch him not. Some faint murmur, indicative of life going on within the house, soothes
him, while he knows not distinctly what it is. He is not
to know anything, not to think of anything. Servants
gliding up or down the distant staircase, treading as upon
velvet, gently keep his ear awake, so long as he troubles
not himself further than with some feeble guess at their
errands.

Exacter knowledge would be a burthen to him: he can
just endure the pressure of conjecture. He opens his eye
faintly at the dull stroke of the muffled knocker, and
closes it again without asking 'who was it?' He is flattered
by a general notion that inquiries are making after him,
but he cares not to know the name of the inquirer. In the
general stillness, and awful hush of the house, he lies in
state, and feels his sovereignty.

To be sick is to enjoy monarchal prerogatives. Compare the silent tread, and quiet ministry, almost by the
eye only, with which he is served—with the careless
demeanour, the unceremonious goings in and out (slap-
ping of doors, or leaving them open) of the very same
attendants, when he is getting a little better—and you
will confess that from the bed of sickness (throne let me
rather call it) to the elbow chair of convalescence is a fall
from dignity, amounting to a deposition.

How convalescence shrinks a man back to his pristine
stature! Where is now the space, which he occupied so
lately, in his own, in the family's eye? The scene of his
regalities, his sick room, which was his presence chamber,

where he lay and acted his despotic fancies—how is it reduced to a common bedroom! The trimness of the very bed has something petty and unmeaning about it. It is *made* every day. How unlike to that wavy, many-furrowed, oceanic surface, which it presented so short a time since, when to *make* it was a service not to be thought of at oftener than three or four day revolutions, when the patient was with pain and grief to be lifted for a little while out of it, to submit to the encroachments of unwelcome neatness, and decencies which his shaken frame deprecated; then to be lifted into it again, for another three or four days' respite, to flounder it out of shape again, while every fresh furrow was a historical record of some shifting posture, some uneasy turning, some seeking for a little ease; and the shrunken skin scarce told a truer story than the crumpled coverlid.

Hushed are those mysterious sighs—those groans—so much more awful while we knew not from what caverns of vast hidden suffering they proceeded. The Lernaean pangs are quenched. The riddle of sickness is solved; and Philoctetes is become an ordinary personage.

Perhaps some relic of the sick man's dream of greatness survives in the still lingering visitations of the medical attendant. But how is he too changed with everything else! Can this be he—this man of news—of chat—of anecdote—of everything but physic—can this be he, who so lately came between the patient and his cruel enemy, as on some solemn embassy from Nature, erecting herself into a high mediating party? Pshaw! 'tis some old woman.

Farewell with him all that made sickness pompous— the spell that hushed the household—the desert-like stillness, felt throughout its inmost chambers—the mute attendance—the inquiry by looks—the still softer delicacies of self-attention—the sole and single eye of distemper alonely fixed upon itself—world-thoughts excluded—the man a world unto himself—his own theatre—

What a speck is he dwindled into!

In this flat swamp of convalescence, left by the ebb of sickness, yet far enough from the terra firma of established health, your note, dear Editor, reached me, requesting— an article. In Articulo Mortis, thought I; but it is something hard—and the quibble, wretched as it was, relieved me. The summons, unseasonable as it appeared, seemed to link me on again to the petty businesses of life, which I had lost sight of; a gentle call to activity, however trivial; a wholesome weaning from that preposterous dream of self-absorption—the puffy state of sickness—in which I confess to have lain so long, insensible to the magazines, and monarchies, of the world alike; to its laws, and to its literature. The hypochondriac flatus is subsiding; the acres, which in imagination I had spread over —for the sick man swells in the sole contemplation of his single sufferings, till he becomes a Tityus to himself—are wasting to a span; and for the giant of self-importance, which I was so lately, you have me once again in my natural pretensions—the lean and meagre figure of your insignificant Essayist.

WILLIAM HAZLITT

THE INDIAN JUGGLERS

COMING forward and seating himself on the ground in his
white dress and tightened turban, the chief of the Indian
Jugglers begins with tossing up two brass balls, which is
what any of us could do, and concludes with keeping up
four at the same time, which is what none of us could do
to save our lives, nor if we were to take our whole lives to
do it in. Is it then a trifling power we see at work, or is it
not something next to miraculous? It is the utmost
stretch of human ingenuity, which nothing but the bend-
ing the faculties of body and mind to it from the tenderest
infancy with incessant, ever anxious application up to
manhood can accomplish or make even a slight approach
to. Man, thou art a wonderful animal, and thy ways past
finding out! Thou canst do strange things, but thou
turnest them to little account! To conceive of this effort
of extraordinary dexterity distracts the imagination and
makes admiration breathless. Yet it costs nothing to the
performer, any more than if it were a mere mechanical
deception with which he had nothing to do but to watch
and laugh at the astonishment of the spectators. A single
error of a hair's-breadth, of the smallest conceivable portion of time, would be fatal: the precision of the movements must be like a mathematical truth, their rapidity
is like lightning. To catch four balls in succession in less
than a second of time, and deliver them back so as to
return with seeming consciousness to the hand again; to
make them revolve round him at certain intervals, like
the planets in their spheres; to make them chase one
another like sparkles of fire, or shoot up like flowers or
meteors; to throw them behind his back and twine them
round his neck like ribbons or like serpents; to do what
appears an impossibility, and to do it with all the ease,
the grace the carelessness imaginable; to laugh at, to

play with the glittering mockeries; to follow them with
his eye as if he could fascinate them with its lambent fire,
or as if he had only to see that they kept time with the
music on the stage—there is something in all this which
he who does not admire may be quite sure he never really
admired anything in the whole course of his life. It is
skill surmounting difficulty, and beauty triumphing over
skill. It seems as if the difficulty once mastered naturally
resolved itself into ease and grace, and as if to be overcome at all, it must be overcome without an effort. The
smallest awkwardness or want of pliancy or self-possession
would stop the whole process. It is the work of witch-
craft, and yet sport for children. Some of the other feats
are quite as curious and wonderful, such as the balancing
the artificial tree and shooting a bird from each branch
through a quill; though none of them has the elegance
or facility of the keeping up of the brass balls. You are in
pain for the result, and glad when the experiment is over;
they are not accompanied with the same unmixed, un-
checked delight as the former; and I would not give much
to be merely astonished without being pleased at the
same time. As to the swallowing of the sword, the police
ought to interfere to prevent it. When I saw the Indian
Juggler do the same things before, his feet were bare, and
he had large rings on the toes, which kept turning round
all the time of the performance, as if they moved of themselves. The hearing a speech in Parliament drawled or
stammered out by the Honourable Member or the Noble
Lord; the ringing the changes on their common-places,
which any one could repeat after them as well as they,
stirs me not a jot, shakes not my good opinion of myself;
but the seeing the Indian Jugglers does. It makes me
ashamed of myself. I ask what there is that I can do as
well as this? Nothing. What have I been doing all my
life? Have I been idle, or have I nothing to show for all
my labour and pains? Or have I passed my time in
pouring words like water into empty sieves, rolling a stone
up a hill and then down again, trying to prove an argument in the teeth of facts, and looking for causes in the

dark and not finding them? Is there no one thing in which I can challenge competition, that I can bring as an instance of exact perfection in which others cannot find a flaw? The utmost I can pretend to is to write a description of what this fellow can do. I can write a book: so can many others who have not even learned to spell. What abortions are these Essays! What errors, what ill-pieced transitions, what crooked reasons, what lame conclusions! How little is made out, and that little how ill! Yet they are the best I can do. I endeavour to recollect all I have ever observed or thought upon a subject, and to express it as nearly as I can. Instead of writing on four subjects at a time, it is as much as I can manage to keep the thread of one discourse clear and unentangled. I have also time on my hands to correct my opinions, and polish my periods; but the one I cannot, and the other I will not do. I am fond of arguing: yet with a good deal of pains and practice it is often as much as I can do to beat my man; though he may be a very indifferent hand. A common fencer would disarm his adversary in the twinkling of an eye, unless he were a professor like himself. A stroke of wit will sometimes produce this effect, but there is no such power or superiority in sense or reasoning. There is no complete mastery of execution to be shown there; and you hardly know the professor from the impudent pretender or the mere clown.[1]

I have always had this feeling of the inefficacy and slow

[1] The celebrated Peter Pindar (Dr. Wolcot) first discovered and brought out the talents of the late Mr. Opie the painter. He was a poor Cornish boy, and was out at work in the fields when the poet went in search of him. 'Well, my lad, can you go and bring me your very best picture?' The other flew like lightning, and soon came back with what he considered as his masterpiece. The stranger looked at it, and the young artist, after waiting for some time without his giving any opinion, at length exclaimed eagerly, 'Well, what do you think of it?' 'Think of it?' said Wolcot, 'why, I think you ought to be ashamed of it—that you, who might do so well, do no better!' The same answer would have applied to this artist's latest performances, that had been suggested by one of his earliest efforts.

progress of intellectual compared to mechanical excellence, and it has always made me somewhat dissatisfied. It is a great many years since I saw Richer, the famous rope-dancer, perform at Sadler's Wells. He was matchless in his art, and added to his extraordinary skill exquisite ease and unaffected, natural grace. I was at that time employed in copying a half-length picture of Sir Joshua Reynolds's; and it put me out of conceit with it. How ill this part was made out in the drawing! How heavy, how slovenly this other was painted! I could not help saying to myself, ' If the rope-dancer had performed his task in this manner, leaving so many gaps and botches in his work, he would have broken his neck long ago; I should never have seen that vigorous elasticity of nerve and precision of movement!' Is it then so easy an undertaking (comparatively) to dance on a tight-rope? Let any one who thinks so get up and try. There is the thing. It is that which at first we cannot do at all which in the end is done to such perfection. To account for this in some degree, I might observe that mechanical dexterity is confined to doing some one particular thing, which you can repeat as often as you please, in which you know whether you succeed or fail, and where the point of perfection consists in succeeding in a given undertaking. In mechanical efforts you improve by perpetual practice, and you do so infallibly, because the object to be attained is not a matter of taste or fancy or opinion, but of actual experiment, in which you must either do the thing or not do it. If a man is put to aim at a mark with a bow and arrow, he must hit it or miss it, that's certain. He cannot deceive himself, and go on shooting wide or falling short, and still fancy that he is making progress. The distinction between right and wrong, between true and false, is here palpable; and he must either correct his aim or persevere in his error with his eyes open, for which there is neither excuse nor temptation. If a man is learning to dance on a rope, if he does not mind what he is about he will break his neck. After that it will be in vain for him to argue that he did not make a false step. His situation is not like that of Goldsmith's pedagogue:

> In argument they own'd his wondrous skill,
> And e'en though vanquish'd, he could argue still.

Danger is a good teacher, and makes apt scholars. So are disgrace, defeat, exposure to immediate scorn and laughter. There is no opportunity in such cases for self-delusion, no idling time away, no being off your guard (or you must take the consequences)—neither is there any room for humour or caprice or prejudice. If the Indian Juggler were to play tricks in throwing up the three case-knives, which keep their positions like the leaves of a crocus in the air, he would cut his fingers. I can make a very bad antithesis without cutting my fingers. The tact of style is more ambiguous than that of double-edged instruments. If the Juggler were told that by flinging himself under the wheels of Juggernaut, when the idol issues forth on a gaudy day, he would immediately be transported into Paradise, he might believe it, and nobody could disprove it. So the Brahmins may say what they please on that subject, may build up dogmas and mysteries without end, and not be detected; but their ingenious countryman cannot persuade the frequenters of the Olympic Theatre that he performs a number of astonishing feats without actually giving proofs of what he says. There is then in this sort of manual dexterity, first a gradual aptitude acquired to a given exertion of muscular power, from constant repetition, and in the next place an exact knowledge how much is still wanting and necessary to be supplied. The obvious test is to increase the effort or nicety of the operation, and still to find it come true. The muscles ply instinctively to the dictates of habit. Certain movements and impressions of the hand and eye, having been repeated together an infinite number of times, are unconsciously but unavoidably cemented into closer and closer union; the limbs require little more than to be put in motion for them to follow a regular track with ease and certainty; so that the mere

intention of the will acts mathematically like touching
the spring of a machine, and you come with Locksley
in *Ivanhoe*, in shooting at a mark, 'to allow for the
wind'.

Further, what is meant by perfection in mechanical
exercises is the performing certain feats to a uniform
nicety, that is, in fact, undertaking no more than you can
perform. You task yourself, the limit you fix is optional,
and no more than human industry and skill can attain
to; but you have no abstract, independent standard of
difficulty or excellence (other than the extent of your own
powers). Thus he who can keep up four brass balls does
this *to perfection*; but he cannot keep up five at the same
instant, and would fail every time he attempted it. That
is, the mechanical performer undertakes to emulate himself, not to equal another. (If two persons play against
each other at any game, one of them necessarily fails.)
But the artist undertakes to imitate another, or to do
what Nature has done, and this it appears is more difficult, viz. to copy what she has set before us in the face
of nature or 'human face divine', entire and without a
blemish, than to keep up four brass balls at the same
instant, for the one is done by the power of human skill
and industry, and the other never was nor will be. Upon
the whole, therefore, I have more respect for Reynolds
than I have for Richer; for, happen how it will, there
have been more people in the world who could dance on
a rope like the one than who could paint like Sir Joshua.
The latter was but a bungler in his profession to the
other, it is true; but then he had a harder taskmaster
to obey, whose will was more wayward and obscure, and
whose instructions it was more difficult to practise. You
can put a child apprentice to a tumbler or rope-dancer
with a comfortable prospect of success, if they are but
sound of wind and limb; but you cannot do the same
thing in painting. The odds are a million to one. You
may make indeed as many H——s and H——s as you
put into that sort of machine, but not one Reynolds
amongst them all, with his grace, his grandeur, his

blandness of gusto, 'in tones and gestures hit', unless you
could make the man over again. To snatch this grace
beyond the reach of art is then the height of art—where
fine art begins, and where mechanical skill ends. The soft
suffusion of the soul, the speechless breathing eloquence,
the looks 'commercing with the skies', the ever-shifting
forms of an eternal principle, that which is seen but for
a moment, but dwells in the heart always, and is only
seized as it passes by strong and secret sympathy, must
be taught by nature and genius, not by rules or study.
It is suggested by feeling, not by laborious microscopic
inspection; in seeking for it without, we lose the harmonious clue to it within; and in aiming to grasp the
substance, we let the very spirit of art evaporate. In a
word, the objects of fine art are not the objects of sight
but as these last are the objects of taste and imagination,
that is, as they appeal to the sense of beauty, of pleasure,
and of power in the human breast, and are explained by
that finer sense, and revealed in their inner structure to
the eye in return. Nature is also a language. Objects,
like words, have a meaning; and the true artist is the
interpreter of this language, which he can only do by
knowing its application to a thousand other objects in
a thousand other situations. Thus the eye is too blind a
guide of itself to distinguish between the warm or cold
tone of a deep-blue sky, but another sense acts as a moni-
tor to it, and does not err. The colour of the leaves in
autumn would be nothing without the feeling that
accompanies it; but it is that feeling that stamps them
on the canvas, faded, seared, blighted, shrinking
from the winter's flaw, and makes the sight as true as
touch—

> And visions, as poetic eyes avow,
> Cling to each leaf and hang on every bough.

The more ethereal, evanescent, more refined and sublime
part of art is the seeing nature through the medium of
sentiment and passion, as each object is a symbol of the
affections and a link in the chain of our endless being.

But the unravelling this mysterious web of thought and feeling is alone in the Muse's gift, namely, in the power of that trembling sensibility which is awake to every change and every modification of its ever-varying impressions, that

Thrills in each nerve, and lives along the line.

This power is indifferently called genius, imagination, feeling, taste; but the manner in which it acts upon the mind can neither be defined by abstract rules, as is the case in science, nor verified by continual, unvarying experiments, as is the case in mechanical performances. The mechanical excellence of the Dutch painters in colouring and handling is that which comes the nearest in fine art to the perfection of certain manual exhibitions of skill. The truth of the effect and the facility with which it is produced are equally admirable. Up to a certain point everything is faultless. The hand and eye have done their part. There is only a want of taste and genius. It is after we enter upon that enchanted ground that the human mind begins to droop and flag as in a strange road, or in a thick mist, benighted and making little way with many attempts and many failures, and that the best of us only escape with half a triumph. The undefined and the imaginary are the regions that we must pass like Satan, difficult and doubtful, 'half flying, half on foot'. The object in sense is a positive thing, and execution comes with practice.

Cleverness is a certain *knack* or aptitude at doing certain things, which depend more on a particular adroitness and off-hand readiness than on force or perseverance, such as making puns, making epigrams, making extempore verses, mimicking the company, mimicking a style, &c. Cleverness is either liveliness and smartness, or something answering to *sleight of hand*, like letting a glass fall sideways off a table, or else a trick, like knowing the secret spring of a watch. Accomplishments are certain external graces, which are to be learnt from others, and which are easily displayed to the admiration of the beholder, viz. dancing, riding, fencing, music, and so on. These ornamental acquirements are only proper to those who are at ease in mind and fortune. I know an individual who if he had been born to an estate of five thousand a year would have been the most accomplished gentleman of the age. He would have been the delight and envy of the circle in which he moved—would have graced by his manners the liberality flowing from the openness of his heart, would have laughed with the women, have argued with the men, have said good things and written agreeable ones, have taken a hand at piquet or the lead at the harpsichord, and have set and sung his own verses—*nugae canorae*—with tenderness and spirit; a Rochester without the vice, a modern Surrey. As it is, all these capabilities of excellence stand in his way. He is too versatile for a professional man, not dull enough for a political drudge, too gay to be happy, too thoughtless to be rich. He wants the enthusiasm of the poet, the severity of the prose-writer, and the application of the man of business. Talent is the capacity of doing anything that depends on application and industry, such as writing a criticism, making a speech, studying the law. Talent differs from genius as voluntary differs from involuntary power. Ingenuity is genius in trifles; greatness is genius in undertakings of much pith and moment. A clever or ingenious man is one who can do anything well, whether it is worth doing or not; a great man is one who can do that which when done is of the highest importance. Themistocles said he could not play on the flute, but that he could make of a small city a great one. This gives one a pretty good idea of the distinction in question.

Greatness is great power, producing great effects. It is not enough that a man has great power in himself; he must show it to all the world in a way that cannot be hid or gainsaid. He must fill up a certain idea in the public mind. I have no other notion of greatness than this twofold definition, great results springing from great inherent energy. The great in visible objects has relation to that which extends over space; the great in mental ones has to do with space and time. No man is truly great who is great only in his lifetime. The test of greatness is the page of history. Nothing can be said to be great that has a distinct limit, or that borders on something evidently greater than itself. Besides, what is short-lived and pampered into mere notoriety is of a gross and vulgar quality in itself. A Lord Mayor is hardly a great man. A city orator or patriot of the day only show, by reaching the height of their wishes, the distance they are at from any true ambition. Popularity is neither fame nor greatness. A king (as such) is not a great man. He has great power, but it is not his own. He merely wields the lever of the state, which a child, an idiot, or a madman can do. It is the office, not the man we gaze at. Any one else in the same situation would be just as much an object of abject curiosity. We laugh at the country girl who having seen a king expressed her disappointment by saying, 'Why, he is only a man!' Yet, knowing this, we run to see a king as if he was something more than a man. To display the greatest powers, unless they are applied to great purposes, makes nothing for the character of greatness. To throw a barleycorn through the eye of a needle, to multiply nine figures by nine in the memory, argues definite dexterity of body and capacity of mind, but nothing comes of either. There is a surprising power at work, but the effects are not proportionate, or such as take hold of the imagination. To impress the idea of power on others, they must be made in some way to feel it. It must be communicated to their understandings in the shape of an increase of knowledge, or it must subdue and overawe them by subjecting their wills. Admiration to be solid and lasting must be founded on proofs from which we have no means of escaping; it is neither a slight nor a voluntary gift. A mathematician who solves a profound problem, a poet who creates an image of beauty in the mind that was not there before, imparts knowledge and power to others, in which his greatness and his fame consists, and on which it reposes. Jedediah Buxton will be forgotten; but Napier's bones will live. Lawgivers, philosophers, founders of religion, conquerors and heroes, inventors and great geniuses in arts and sciences, are great men, for they are great public benefactors, or formidable scourges to mankind. Among ourselves, Shakespeare, Newton, Bacon, Milton, Cromwell, were great men, for they showed great power by acts and thoughts, which have not yet been consigned to oblivion. They must needs be men of lofty stature, whose shadows lengthen out to remote posterity. A great farce-writer may be a great man; for Molière was but a great farce-writer. In my mind, the author of *Don Quixote* was a great man. So have there been many others. A great chess-player is not a great man, for he leaves the world as he found it. No act terminating in itself constitutes greatness. This will apply to all displays of power or trials of skill which are confined to the momentary, individual effort, and construct no permanent image or trophy of themselves without them. Is not an actor then a great man, because 'he dies and leaves the world no copy'? I must make an exception for Mrs. Siddons, or else give up my definition of greatness for her sake. A man at the top of his profession is not therefore a great man. He is great in his way, but that is all, unless he shows the marks of a great moving intellect, so that we trace the master-mind, and can sympathize with the springs that urge him on. The rest is but a craft or *mystery*. John Hunter was a great man—*that* any one might see without the smallest skill in surgery. His style and manner showed the man. He would set about cutting up the carcass of a whale with the same greatness of gusto that Michaelangelo would have hewn a block of marble. Lord Nelson was a great naval commander; but for myself, I have not much opinion of a seafaring life. Sir Humphry Davy is a great chemist, but I am not sure that he is a great man. I am not a bit the wiser for any of his discoveries, nor ever met with any one that was. But it is in the nature of greatness to propagate an idea of itself, as wave impels wave, circle without circle. It is a contradiction in terms for a coxcomb to be a great man. A really great man has always an idea of something greater than himself. I have observed that certain sectaries and polemical writers have no higher compliment to pay their most shining lights than to say that 'Such a one was a considerable man in his day'. Some new elucidation of a text sets aside the authority of the old interpretation, and a 'great scholar's memory outlives him half a century', at the utmost. A rich man is not a great man, except to his dependants and his steward. A lord is a great man in the idea we have of his ancestry, and probably of himself, if we know nothing of him but his title. I have heard a story of two bishops, one of whom said (speaking of St. Peter's at Rome) that when he first entered it, he was rather awe-struck, but that as he walked up it, his mind seemed to swell and dilate with it, and at last to fill the whole building: the other said that as he saw more of it, he appeared to himself to grow less and less every step he took, and in the end to dwindle into nothing. This was in some respects a striking picture of a great and little mind—for greatness sympathizes with greatness, and littleness shrinks into itself. The one might have become a Wolsey; the other was only fit to become a Mendicant Friar—or there might have been court reasons for making him a bishop. The French have to me a character of littleness in all about them; but they have produced three great men that belong to every country—Molière, Rabelais, and Montaigne.

To return from this digression, and conclude the essay. A singular instance of manual dexterity was shown in the person of the late John Cavanagh, whom I have several times seen. His death was celebrated at the time in an article in the *Examiner* newspaper (Feb. 7, 1819), written apparently between jest and earnest; but as it is *pat* to our purpose, and falls in with my own way of considering such subjects, I shall here take leave to quote it.

'Died at his house in Burbage Street, St. Giles's, John Cavanagh, the famous hand fives-player. When a person dies who does any one thing better than any one else in the world, which so many others are trying to do well, it leaves a gap in society. It is not likely that any one will now see the game of fives played in its perfection for many years to come—for Cavanagh is dead, and has not left his peer behind him. It may be said that there are things of more importance than striking a ball against a wall—there are things indeed that make more noise and do as little good, such as making war and peace, making speeches and answering them, making verses and blotting them, making money and throwing it away. But the game of fives is what no one despises who has ever played at it. It is the finest exercise for the body, and the best relaxation for the mind. The Roman poet said that "Care mounted behind the horseman and stuck to his skirts". But this remark would not have applied to the fives-player. He who takes to playing at fives is twice young. He feels neither the past nor future "in the instant". Debts, taxes, "domestic treason, foreign levy, nothing can touch him further". He has no other wish, no other thought, from the moment the game begins, but that of striking the ball, of placing it, of *making* it! This Cavanagh was sure to do. Whenever he touched the ball there was an end of the chase. His eye was certain, his hand fatal, his presence of mind complete. He could do what he pleased, and he always knew exactly what to do. He saw the whole game, and played it; took instant advantage of his adversary's weakness, and recovered balls, as if by a miracle and from sudden thought, that every one gave for lost. He had equal power and skill, quickness and judgement. He could either outwit his antagonist by finesse, or beat him by main strength. Sometimes, when he seemed preparing to send the ball with the full swing of his arm, he would by a slight turn of his wrist drop it within an inch of the line. In general, the ball came from his hand, as if from a racket, in a straight, horizontal line; so that it was in vain to attempt to overtake or stop it. As it was said of a great orator that he never was at a loss for a word, and for the properest word, so Cavanagh always could tell the degree of force necessary to be given to a ball, and the precise direction in which it should be sent. He did his work with the greatest ease; never took more pains than was necessary; and, while others were fagging themselves to death, was as cool and collected as if he had just entered the court. His style of play was as remarkable as his power of execution. He had no affectation, no trifling. He did not throw away the game to show off an attitude or try an experiment. He was a fine, sensible, manly player, who did what he could, but that was more than any one else could even affect to do. His blows were not undecided and ineffectual— lumbering like Mr. Wordsworth's epic poetry, nor wavering like Mr. Coleridge's lyric prose, nor short of the mark like Mr. Brougham's speeches, nor wide of it like Mr. Canning's wit, nor foul like the *Quarterly*, nor *let* balls like the *Edinburgh Review*. Cobbett and Junius together would have made a Cavanagh. He was the best *up-hill* player in the world; even when his adversary was fourteen, he would play on the same or better, and as he never flung away the game through carelessness and conceit, he never gave it up through laziness or want of heart. The only peculiarity of his play was that he never *volleyed*, but let the balls hop; but if they rose an inch from the ground he never missed having them. There was not only nobody equal, but nobody second to him. It is supposed that he could give any other player half the game, or beat them with his left hand. His service was tremendous. He once played Woodward and Meredith together (two of the best players in England) in the Fives-court, St. Martin's Street, and made seven-and-twenty aces following by services alone—a thing unheard of. He another time played Peru, who was considered a first-rate fives-player, a match of the best out of five games, and in the three first games, which of course decided the match, Peru got only one ace. Cavanagh was an Irishman by birth, and a house-painter by profession. He had once laid aside his working-dress, and walked up, in his smartest clothes, to the Rosemary Branch to have an afternoon's pleasure. A person accosted him, and asked him if he would have a game. So they agreed to play for half-a-crown a game and a bottle of cider. The first game began—it was seven, eight, ten, thirteen, fourteen, all. Cavanagh won it. The next was the same. They played on, and each game was hardly contested. "There," said the unconscious fives-player, "there was a stroke that Cavanagh could not take: I never played better in my life, and yet I can't win a game. I don't know how it is." However, they played on, Cavanagh winning every game, and the by-standers drinking the cider and laughing all the time. In the twelfth game, when Cavanagh was only four, and the stranger thirteen, a person came in and said, "What! are you here, Cavanagh?" The words were no sooner pro-nounced than the astonished player let the ball drop from his hand, and saying, "What! have I been breaking my heart all this time to beat Cavanagh?" refused to make another effort. "And yet, I give you my word," said Cavanagh, telling the story with some triumph, "I played all the while with my clenched fist." He used frequently to play matches at Copenhagen House for wagers and dinners. The wall against which they play is the same that supports the kitchen-chimney, and when the wall re-sounded louder than usual, the cooks exclaimed, "Those are the Irishman's balls", and the joints trembled on the spit! Goldsmith consoled himself that there were places where he too was admired: and Cavanagh was the ad-miration of all the fives-courts where he ever played. Mr. Powell, when he played matches in the court in St. Martin's Street, used to fill his gallery at half-a-crown a head with amateurs and admirers of talent in whatever department it is shown. He could not have shown him-self in any ground in England but he would have been immediately surrounded with inquisitive gazers, trying to find out in what part of his frame his unrivalled skill lay, as politicians wonder to see the balance of Europe suspended in Lord Castlereagh's face, and admire the trophies of the British Navy lurking under Mr. Croker's hanging brow. Now Cavanagh was as good-looking a man as the Noble Lord, and much better looking than the

Right Hon. Secretary. He had a clear, open countenance, and did not look sideways or down, like Mr. Murray the bookseller. He was a young fellow of sense, humour, and courage. He once had a quarrel with a waterman at Hungerford Stairs, and, they say, served him out in great style. In a word, there are hundreds at this day who cannot mention his name without admiration, as the best fives-player that perhaps ever lived (the greatest excellence of which they have any notion)—and the noisy shout of the ring happily stood him in stead of the unheard voice of posterity! The only person who seems to have excelled as much in another way as Cavanagh did in his was the late John Davies, the racket-player. It was remarked of him that he did not seem to follow the ball, but the ball seemed to follow him. Give him a foot of wall, and he was sure to make the ball. The four best racket-players of that day were Jack Spines, Jem Harding, Armitage, and Church. Davies could give any one of these two hands a time, that is, half the game, and each of these, at their best, could give the best player now in London the same odds. Such are the gradations in all exertions of human skill and art. He once played four capital players together, and beat them. He was also a first-rate tennis-player, and an excellent fives-player. In the Fleet or King's Bench he would have stood against Powell, who was reckoned the best open-ground player of his time. This last-mentioned player is at present the keeper of the Fives-Court, and we might recommend to him for a motto over his door, "Who enters here, forgets himself, his country, and his friends." And the best of it is, that by the calculation of the odds, none of the three are worth remembering! Cavanagh died from the bursting of a blood-vessel, which prevented him from playing for the last two or three years. This, he was often heard to say, he thought hard upon him. He was fast recovering, however, when he was suddenly carried off, to the regret of all who knew him. As Mr. Peel made it a qualification of the present Speaker, Mr. Manners Sutton, that he was an excellent moral character, so

Jack Cavanagh was a zealous Catholic, and could not be persuaded to eat meat on a Friday, the day on which he died. We have paid this willing tribute to his memory.

> Let no rude hand deface it,
> And his forlorn *Hic Jacet*.'

THOMAS DE QUINCEY

THE ENGLISH MAIL-COACH

THE GLORY OF MOTION

SOME twenty or more years before I matriculated at Oxford, Mr. Palmer, at that time M.P. for Bath, had accomplished two things, very hard to do on our little planet, the Earth, however cheap they may be held by eccentric people in comets—he had invented mail-coaches, and he had married the daughter of a duke. He was, therefore, just twice as great a man as Galileo, who did certainly invent (or, which is the same thing, discover) the satellites of Jupiter, those very next things extant to mail-coaches in the two capital pretensions of speed and keeping time, but, on the other hand, who did *not* marry the daughter of a duke.

These mail-coaches, as organized by Mr. Palmer, are entitled to a circumstantial notice from myself, having had so large a share in developing the anarchies of my subsequent dreams; an agency which they accomplished, first, through velocity, at that time unprecedented—for they first revealed the glory of motion; secondly, through grand effects for the eye between lamplight and the darkness upon solitary roads; thirdly, through animal beauty and power so often displayed in the class of horses selected for this mail service; fourthly, through the conscious presence of a central intellect, that, in the midst of vast distances—of storms, of darkness, of danger—overruled all obstacles into one steady co-operation to a national result. For my own feeling this post-office service spoke as by some mighty orchestra, where a thousand instruments, all disregarding each other, and so far in danger of discord, yet all obedient as slaves to the supreme *bâton* of some great leader, terminate in a perfection of harmony like that of heart, brain, and lungs, in a healthy animal organization. But, finally, that particular element in this

E

whole combination which most impressed myself, and
through which it is that to this hour Mr. Palmer's mail-
coach system tyrannizes over my dreams by terror and
terrific beauty, lay in the awful *political* mission which at
that time it fulfilled. The mail-coach it was that distributed over the face of the land, like the opening of
apocalyptic vials, the heart-shaking news of Trafalgar,
of Salamanca, of Vittoria, of Waterloo. These were the
harvests that, in the grandeur of their reaping, redeemed
the tears and blood in which they had been sown. Neither
was the meanest peasant so much below the grandeur and
the sorrow of the times as to confound battles such as
these, which were gradually moulding the destinies of
Christendom, with the vulgar conflicts of ordinary war-
fare, so often no more than gladiatorial trials of national
prowess. The victories of England in this stupendous
contest rose of themselves as natural *Te Deums* to heaven;
and it was felt by the thoughtful that such victories, at
such a crisis of general prostration, were not more
beneficial to ourselves than finally to France, our enemy,
and to the nations of all western or central Europe,
through whose pusillanimity it was that the French
domination had prospered.

The mail-coach, as the national organ for publishing
these mighty events thus diffusively influential, became
itself a spiritualized and glorified object to an impassioned
heart; and naturally, in the Oxford of that day, *all* hearts
were impassioned, as being all (or nearly all) in *early* manhood. In most universities there is one single college; in
Oxford there were five-and-twenty, all of which were
peopled by young men, the *élite* of their own generation;
not boys, but men; none under eighteen. In some of these
many colleges the custom permitted the student to keep
what are called 'short terms'; that is, the four terms of
Michaelmas, Lent, Easter, and Act, were kept by a
residence, in the aggregate, of ninety-one days, or
thirteen weeks. Under this interrupted residence it was
possible that a student might have a reason for going
down to his home four times in the year. This made eight

journeys to and fro. But, as these homes lay dispersed
through all the shires of the island, and most of us dis-
dained all coaches except his Majesty's mail, no city out
of London could pretend to so extensive a connexion with
Mr. Palmer's establishment as Oxford. Three mails, at
the least, I remember as passing every day through
Oxford, and benefitting by my personal patronage—viz.
the Worcester, the Gloucester, and the Holyhead mail.
Naturally, therefore, it became a point of some interest
with us, whose journeys revolved every six weeks on an
average, to look a little into the executive details of the
system. With some of these Mr. Palmer had no concern;
they rested upon by-laws enacted by posting-houses for
their own benefit, and upon other by-laws, equally stern,
enacted by the inside passengers for the illustration of
their own haughty exclusiveness. These last were of a
nature to rouse our scorn, from which the transition was
not very long to systematic mutiny. Up to this time, say
1804, or 1805 (the year of Trafalgar), it had been the fixed
assumption of the four inside people (as an old tradition
of all public carriages derived from the reign of Charles II),
that they, the illustrious quaternion, constituted a
porcelain variety of the human race, whose dignity would
have been compromised by exchanging one word of
civility with the three miserable delf-ware outsides.
Even to have kicked an outsider might have been held
to attaint the foot concerned in that operation; so that,
perhaps, it would have required an act of parliament to
restore its purity of blood. What words, then, could
express the horror, and the sense of treason, in that case,
which *had* happened, where all three outsides (the trinity
of pariahs) made a vain attempt to sit down at the same
breakfast-table or dinner-table with the consecrated
four? I myself witnessed such an attempt; and on that
occasion a benevolent old gentleman endeavoured to
soothe his three holy associates, by suggesting that, if the
outsides were indicted for this criminal attempt at the
next assizes, the court would regard it as a case of lunacy,
or *delirium tremens*, rather than of treason. England owes

much of her grandeur to the depth of the aristocratic
element in her social composition, when pulling against
her strong democracy. I am not the man to laugh at it.
But sometimes, undoubtedly, it expressed itself in comic
shapes. The course taken with the infatuated outsiders,
in the particular attempt which I have noticed, was, that
the waiter, beckoning them away from the privileged
salle-à-manger, sang out, 'This way, my good men,' and
then enticed these good men away to the kitchen. But
that plan had not always answered. Sometimes, though
rarely, cases occurred where the intruders, being stronger
than usual, or more vicious than usual, resolutely refused
to budge, and so far carried their point, as to have a
separate table arranged for themselves in a corner of the
general room. Yet, if an Indian screen could be found
ample enough to plant them out from the very eyes of the
high table, or dais, it then became possible to assume as
a fiction of law—that the three delf fellows, after all,
were not present. They could be ignored by the porcelain
men, under the maxim, that objects not appearing, and
not existing, are governed by the same logical construc-
tion.

Such being, at that time, the usages of mail-coaches,
what was to be done by us of young Oxford? We,
the most aristocratic of people, who were addicted to the
practice of looking down superciliously even upon the
insides themselves as often very questionable characters
—were we, by voluntarily going outside, to court indigni-
ties? If our dress and bearing sheltered us, generally,
from the suspicion of being 'raff' (the name at that period
for 'snobs'), we really *were* such constructively, by the
place we assumed. If we did not submit to the deep
shadow of eclipse, we entered at least the skirts of its
penumbra. And the analogy of theatres was valid against
us, where no man can complain of the annoyances
incident to the pit or gallery, having his instant remedy
in paying the higher price of the boxes. But the sound-
ness of this analogy we disputed. In the case of the
theatre it cannot be pretended that the inferior situations

have any separate attractions, unless the pit may be
supposed to have an advantage for the purposes of the
critic or the dramatic reporter. But the critic or reporter
is a rarity. For most people the sole benefit is in the
price. Now, on the contrary, the outside of the mail had
its own incommunicable advantages. These we could not
forego. The higher price we would willingly have paid,
but not the price connected with the condition of riding
inside; which condition we pronounced insufferable. The
air, the freedom of prospect, the proximity to the horses,
the elevation of seat—these were what we required; but,
above all, the certain anticipation of purchasing occasional
opportunities of driving.

Such was the difficulty which pressed us; and under the
coercion of this difficulty we instituted a searching inquiry
into the true quality and valuation of the different apart-
ments about the mail. We conducted this inquiry on
metaphysical principles; and it was ascertained satis-
factorily that the roof of the coach, which by some weak
men had been called the attics, and by some the garrets,
was in reality the drawing-room; in which drawing-room
the box was the chief ottoman or sofa; whilst it appeared
that the *inside*, which had been traditionally regarded as
the only room tenantable by gentlemen, was, in fact, the
coal-cellar in disguise.

Great wits jump. The very same idea had not long
before struck the celestial intellect of China. Amongst
the presents carried out by our first embassy to that
country was a state-coach. It had been specially selected
as a personal gift by George III; but the exact mode of
using it was an intense mystery to Pekin. The Ambas-
sador, indeed (Lord Macartney), had made some imperfect explanations upon this point; but, as his Excellency
communicated these in a diplomatic whisper, at the very
moment of his departure, the celestial intellect was very
feebly illuminated, and it became necessary to call a
Cabinet Council on the grand state question, 'Where was
the Emperor to sit?' The hammer-cloth happened to be
unusually gorgeous; and partly on that consideration,

but partly also because the box offered the most elevated
seat, was nearest to the moon, and undeniably went foremost, it was resolved by acclamation that the box was the
Imperial throne, and for the scoundrel who drove, he
might sit where he could find a perch. The horses, therefore, being harnessed, solemnly his Imperial Majesty
ascended his new English throne under a flourish of
trumpets, having the First Lord of the Treasury on his
right hand, and the Chief Jester on his left. Pekin gloried
in the spectacle; and in the whole flowery people, constructively present by representation, there was but one
discontented person, and *that* was the coachman. This
mutinous individual audaciously shouted, 'Where am *I*
to sit?' But the Privy Council, incensed by his disloyalty,
unanimously opened the door, and kicked him into the
inside. He had all the inside places to himself; but such
is the rapacity of ambition, that he was still dissatisfied.
'I say,' he cried out in an extempore petition, addressed
to the Emperor through the window—'I say, how am I
to catch hold of the reins?'—'Anyhow,' was the Imperial
answer; 'don't trouble *me*, man, in my glory. How catch
the reins? Why, through the windows, through the key-
holes—*any*how.' Finally this contumacious coachman
lengthened the check-strings into a sort of jury-reins,
communicating with the horses; with these he drove as
steadily as Pekin had any right to expect. The Emperor
returned after the briefest of circuits; he descended in
great pomp from his throne, with the severest resolution
never to remount it. A public thanksgiving was ordered
for his Majesty's happy escape from the disease of broken
neck; and the state-coach was dedicated thenceforward
as a votive offering to the god Fo-Fo—whom the learned
more accurately called Fi-Fi.

A revolution of this same Chinese character did young
Oxford of that era effect in the constitution of mail-coach
society. It was a perfect French revolution; and we had
good reason to say, *Ça ira*. In fact, it soon became *too*
popular. The 'public'—a well-known character, particularly disagreeable, though slightly respectable, and

notorious for affecting the chief seats in synagogues—
had at first loudly opposed this revolution; but when the
opposition showed itself to be ineffectual, our disagreeable
friend went into it with headlong zeal. At first it was a
sort of race between us; and, as the public is usually from
thirty to fifty years old, naturally we of young Oxford,
that averaged about twenty, had the advantage. Then the
public took to bribing, giving fees to horse-keepers, &c.,
who hired out their persons as warming-pans on the box-
seat. *That*, you know, was shocking to all moral sensibilities. Come to bribery, said we, and there is an end to
all morality, Aristotle's, Zeno's, Cicero's, or anybody's.
And, besides, of what use was it? For *we* bribed also.
And as our bribes to those of the public were as five
shillings to sixpence, here again young Oxford had the
advantage. But the contest was ruinous to the principles
of the stables connected with the mails. This whole
corporation was constantly bribed, rebribed, and often
sur-rebribed; a mail-coach yard was like the hustings in a
contested election; and a horse-keeper, ostler, or helper,
was held by the philosophical at that time to be the most
corrupt character in the nation.

There was an impression upon the public mind, natural
enough from the continually augmenting velocity of the
mail, but quite erroneous, that an outside seat on this
class of carriages was a post of danger. On the contrary,
I maintained that, if a man had become nervous from
some gipsy prediction in his childhood, allocating to a
particular moon now approaching some unknown danger,
and he should inquire earnestly, 'Whither can I fly for
shelter? Is a prison the safest retreat? or a lunatic
hospital? or the British Museum?' I should have replied,
'Oh, no; I'll tell you what to do. Take lodgings for the
next forty days on the box of his Majesty's mail. Nobody
can touch you there. If it is by bills at ninety days after
date that you are made unhappy—if noters and protesters
are the sort of wretches whose astrological shadows
darken the house of life—then note you what I vehemently
protest—viz. that no matter though the sheriff and under-

sheriff in every county should be running after you with
his *posse*, touch a hair of your head he cannot whilst you
keep house, and have your legal domicile on the box of
the mail. It is felony to stop the mail; even the sheriff
cannot do that. And an *extra* touch of the whip to the
leaders (no great matter if it grazes the sheriff) at any
time guarantees your safety.' In fact, a bedroom in a
quiet house seems a safe enough retreat, yet it is liable to
its own notorious nuisances—to robbers by night, to rats,
to fire. But the mail laughs at these terrors. To robbers,
the answer is packed up and ready for delivery in the
barrel of the guard's blunderbuss. Rats again!—there
are none about mail-coaches, any more than snakes in
Von Troil's *Iceland*; except, indeed, now and then a parliamentary rat, who always hides his shame in what I have
shown to be the 'coal-cellar'. And as to fire, I never knew
but one in a mail-coach, which was in the Exeter mail, and
caused by an obstinate sailor bound to Devonport. Jack,
making light of the law and the lawgiver that had set
their faces against his offence, insisted on taking up a
forbidden seat in the rear of the roof, from which he could
exchange his own yarns with those of the guard. No
greater offence was then known to mail-coaches; it was
treason, it was *laesa majestas*, it was by tendency arson;
and the ashes of Jack's pipe, falling amongst the straw of
the hinder boot containing the mail-bags, raised a flame
which (aided by the wind of our motion) threatened a
revolution in the republic of letters. Yet even this left
the sanctity of the box unviolated. In dignified repose the
coachman and myself sat on, resting with benign com-
posure upon our knowledge that the fire would have to
burn its way through four inside passengers before it
could reach ourselves. I remarked to the coachman, with
a quotation from Virgil's *Aeneid* really too hackneyed—

> Jam proximus ardet
> Ucalegon.

But, recollecting that the Virgilian part of the coachman's
education might have been neglected, I interpreted so far

as to say that perhaps at that moment the flames were catching hold of our worthy brother and inside passenger, Ucalegon. The coachman made no answer, which is my own way when a stranger addresses me either in Syriac or in Coptic, but by his faint sceptical smile he seemed to insinuate that he knew better; for that Ucalegon, as it happened, was not in the way-bill, and therefore could not have been booked.

No dignity is perfect which does not at some point ally itself with the mysterious. The connexion of the mail with the State and the Executive Government—a connexion obvious, but yet not strictly defined—gave to the whole mail establishment an official grandeur which did us service on the roads, and invested us with seasonable terrors. Not the less impressive were those terrors, because their legal limits were imperfectly ascertained. Look at those turnpike gates; with what deferential hurry, with what an obedient start, they fly open at our approach! Look at that long line of carts and carters ahead, audaciously usurping the very crest of the road. Ah! traitors, they do not hear us as yet; but, as soon as the dreadful blast of our horn reaches them with proclamation of our approach, see with what frenzy of trepidation they fly to their horses' heads, and deprecate our wrath by the precipitation of their crane-neck quarterings. Treason they feel to be their crime; each individual carter feels himself under the ban of confiscation and attainder; his blood is attainted through six generations; and nothing is wanting but the headsman and his axe, the block and the saw-dust, to close up the vista of his horrors. What! shall it be within benefit of clergy to delay the King's message on the high road?—to interrupt the great respirations, ebb and flood, *systole* and *diastole*, of the national intercourse?—to endanger the safety of tidings, running day and night between all nations and languages? Or can it be fancied, amongst the weakest of men, that the bodies of the criminals will be given up to their widows for Christian burial? Now the doubts which were raised as to our powers did more to wrap them in terror, by wrapping them in uncertainty, than could have been effected by the sharpest definitions of the law from the Quarter Sessions. We, on our parts (we, the collective mail, I mean), did our utmost to exalt the idea of our privileges by the insolence with which we wielded them. Whether this insolence rested upon law that gave it a sanction, or upon conscious power that haughtily dispensed with that sanction, equally it spoke from a potential station; and the agent, in each particular insolence of the moment, was viewed reverentially, as one having authority.

Sometimes after breakfast his Majesty's mail would become frisky; and, in its difficult wheelings amongst the intricacies of early markets, it would upset an apple-cart, a cart loaded with eggs, &c. Huge was the affliction and dismay, awful was the smash. I, as far as possible, endeavoured in such a case to represent the conscience and moral sensibilities of the mail; and, when wildernesses of eggs were lying poached under our horses' hoofs, then would I stretch forth my hands in sorrow, saying (in words too celebrated at that time, from the false echoes of Marengo), 'Ah! wherefore have we not time to weep over you?' which was evidently impossible, since, in fact, we had not time to laugh over them. Tied to post-office allowance, in some cases of fifty minutes for eleven miles, could the royal mail pretend to undertake the offices of sympathy and condolence? Could it be expected to provide tears for the accidents of the road? If even it seemed to trample on humanity, it did so, I felt, in discharge of its own more peremptory duties.

Upholding the morality of the mail, *a fortiori* I upheld its rights; as a matter of duty, I stretched to the uttermost its privilege of Imperial precedency, and astonished weak minds by the feudal powers which I hinted to be lurking constructively in the charters of this proud establishment. Once I remember being on the box of the Holyhead mail, between Shrewsbury and Oswestry, when a tawdry thing from Birmingham, some 'Tallyho' or 'Highflyer', all flaunting with green and gold, came up alongside of us.

What a contrast to our royal simplicity of form and colour in this plebeian wretch! The single ornament on our dark ground of chocolate colour was the mighty shield of the Imperial arms, but emblazoned in proportions as modest as a signet-ring bears to a seal of office. Even this was displayed only on a single panel, whispering, rather than proclaiming, our relations to the mighty State; whilst the beast from Birmingham, our green-and-gold friend from false, fleeting, perjured Brummagem, had as much writing and painting on its sprawling flanks as would have puzzled a decipherer from the tombs of Luxor. For some time this Birmingham machine ran along by our side—a piece of familiarity that already of itself seemed to me sufficiently Jacobinical. But all at once a movement of the horses announced a desperate intention of leaving us behind. 'Do you see *that*?' I said to the coachman. 'I see,' was his short answer. He was wide awake, yet he waited longer than seemed prudent; for the horses of our audacious opponent had a disagreeable air of freshness and power. But his motive was loyal; his wish was that the Birmingham conceit should be full-blown before he froze it. When *that* seemed right, he unloosed, or, to speak by a stronger word, he *sprang*, his known resources: he slipped our royal horses like cheetahs, or hunting-leopards, after the affrighted game. How they could retain such a reserve of fiery power, after the work they had accomplished, seemed hard to explain. But on our side, besides the physical superiority, was a tower of moral strength, namely, the King's name, 'which they upon the adverse faction wanted'. Passing them without an effort, as it seemed, we threw them into the rear with so lengthening an interval between us, as proved in itself the bitterest mockery of their presumption; whilst our guard blew back a shattering blast of triumph, that was really too painfully full of derision.

I mention this little incident for its connexion with what followed. A Welsh rustic, sitting behind me, asked if I had not felt my heart burn within me during the progress of the race. I said, with philosophic calmness, *No*;

because we were not racing with a mail, so that no glory could be gained. In fact, it was sufficiently mortifying that such a Birmingham thing should dare to challenge us. The Welshman replied that he didn't see *that*; for that a cat might look at a king, and a Brummagem coach might lawfully race the Holyhead mail. '*Race* us, if you like,' I replied, 'though even *that* has an air of sedition, but not *beat* us. This would have been treason; and for its own sake I am glad that the "Tallyho" was disappointed.' So dissatisfied did the Welshman seem with this opinion, that at last I was obliged to tell him a very fine story from one of our elder dramatists—viz. that once, in some far oriental kingdom, when the Sultan of all the land, with his princes, ladies, and chief omrahs, were flying their falcons, a hawk suddenly flew at a majestic eagle; and in defiance of the eagle's natural advantages, in contempt also of the eagle's traditional royalty, and before the whole assembled field of astonished spectators from Agra and Lahore, killed the eagle on the spot. Amazement seized the Sultan at the unequal contest, and burning admiration for its unparalleled result. He commanded that the hawk should be brought before him; he caressed the bird with enthusiasm; and he ordered that, for the commemoration of his matchless courage, a diadem of gold and rubies should be solemnly placed on the hawk's head; but then that, immediately after this solemn coronation, the bird should be led off to execution, as the most valiant indeed of traitors, but not the less a traitor, as having dared to rise rebelliously against his liege lord and anointed sovereign, the eagle. 'Now,' said I to the Welshman, 'to you and me, as men of refined sensibilities, how painful it would have been that this poor Brummagem brute, the "Tallyho", in the impossible case of a victory over us, should have been crowned with Birmingham tinsel, with paste diamonds, and Roman pearls, and then led off to instant execution.' The Welshman doubted if that could be warranted by law. And when I hinted at the 6th of Edward Longshanks, chap. 18, for regulating the precedency of coaches,

as being probably the statute relied on for the capital
punishment of such offences, he replied drily that, if the
attempt to pass a mail really were treasonable, it was a
pity that the 'Tallyho' appeared to have so imperfect an
acquaintance with law.

The modern modes of travelling cannot compare with
the old mail-coach system in grandeur and power. They
boast of more velocity, not, however, as a consciousness,
but as a fact of our lifeless knowledge, resting upon *alien*
evidence; as, for instance, because somebody *says* that we
have gone fifty miles in the hour, though we are far from
feeling it as a personal experience, or upon the evidence
of a result, as that actually we find ourselves in York four
hours after leaving London. Apart from such an asser-
tion, or such a result, I myself am little aware of the pace.
But, seated on the old mail-coach, we needed no evidence
out of ourselves to indicate the velocity. On this system
the word was not 'magna loquimur', as upon railways,
but 'vivimus'. Yes, 'magna *vivimus*'; we do not make
verbal ostentation of our grandeurs, we realize our grandeurs in act, and in the very experience of life. The vital
experience of the glad animal sensibilities made doubts
impossible on the question of our speed; we heard our
speed, we saw it, we felt it as a thrilling; and this speed
was not the product of blind insensate agencies, that had
no sympathy to give, but was incarnated in the fiery
eyeballs of the noblest amongst brutes, in his dilated
nostril, spasmodic muscles, and thunder-beating hoofs.
The sensibility of the horse, uttering itself in the maniac
light of his eye, might be the last vibration of such a movement; the glory of Salamanca might be the first. But the
intervening links that connected them, that spread the
earthquake of battle into the eyeball of the horse, were
the heart of man and its electric thrillings—kindling in
the rapture of the fiery strife, and then propagating its
own tumults by contagious shouts and gestures to the
heart of his servant the horse.

But now, on the new system of travelling, iron tubes
and boilers have disconnected man's heart from the

ministers of his locomotion. Nile nor Trafalgar has power
to raise an extra bubble in a steam-kettle. The galvanic
cycle is broken up for ever; man's imperial nature no
longer sends itself forward through the electric sensibility
of the horse; the inter-agencies are gone in the mode of
communication between the horse and his master, out of
which grew so many aspects of sublimity under accidents
of mists that hid, or sudden blazes that revealed, of mobs
that agitated, or midnight solitudes that awed. Tidings,
fitted to convulse all nations, must henceforwards travel
by culinary process; and the trumpet that once announced
from afar the laurelled mail, heart-shaking, when heard
screaming on the wind, and proclaiming itself through
the darkness to every village or solitary house on its
route, has now given way for ever to the pot-wallopings
of the boiler.

Thus have perished multiform openings for public
expressions of interest, scenical yet natural, in great
national tidings; for revelations of faces and groups that
could not offer themselves amongst the fluctuating mobs
of a railway station. The gatherings of gazers about a
laurelled mail had one centre, and acknowledged one sole
interest. But the crowds attending at a railway station
have as little unity as running water, and own as many
centres as there are separate carriages in the train.

How else, for example, than as a constant watcher for
the dawn, and for the London mail that in summer
months entered about daybreak amongst the lawny
thickets of Marlborough forest, couldst thou, sweet Fanny
of the Bath road, have become the glorified inmate of
my dreams? Yet Fanny, as the loveliest young woman
for face and person that perhaps in my whole life I have
beheld, merited the station which even now, from a distance of forty years, she holds in my dreams; yes, though
by links of natural association she brings along with her
a troop of dreadful creatures, fabulous and not fabulous,
that are more abominable to the heart than Fanny and
the dawn are delightful.

Miss Fanny of the Bath road, strictly speaking, lived

at a mile's distance from that road; but came so continually to meet the mail, that I on my frequent transits
rarely missed her, and naturally connected her image with
the great thoroughfare where only I had ever seen her.
Why she came so punctually, I do not exactly know; but
I believe with some burden of commissions to be executed
in Bath, which had gathered to her own residence as a
central rendezvous for converging them. The mail-coach-
man who drove the Bath mail, and wore the royal livery,
happened to be Fanny's grandfather. A good man he
was, that loved his beautiful granddaughter; and, loving
her wisely, was vigilant over her deportment in any case
where young Oxford might happen to be concerned. Did
my vanity then suggest that I myself, individually, could
fall within the line of his terrors? Certainly not, as regarded any physical pretensions that I could plead; for
Fanny (as a chance passenger from her own neighbourhood once told me) counted in her train a hundred and
ninety-nine professed admirers, if not open aspirants to
her favour; and probably not one of the whole brigade
but excelled myself in personal advantages. Ulysses even,
with the unfair advantage of his accursed bow, could
hardly have undertaken that amount of suitors. So the
danger might have seemed slight—only that woman is
universally aristocratic; it is amongst her nobilities of
heart that she *is* so. Now, the aristocratic distinctions
in my favour might easily with Miss Fanny have com-
pensated my physical deficiencies. Did I then make love
to Fanny? Why, yes; about as much love as one *could*
make whilst the mail was changing horses—a process
which, ten years later, did not occupy above eighty
seconds; but *then*—viz. about Waterloo—it occupied five
times eighty. Now, four hundred seconds offer a field
quite ample enough for whispering into a young woman's
ear a great deal of truth, and (by way of parenthesis)
some trifle of falsehood. Grandpapa did right, therefore,
to watch me. And yet, as happens too often to the
grandpapas of earth, in a contest with the admirers of
granddaughters, how vainly would he have watched me

had I meditated any evil whispers to Fanny! She, it is
my belief, would have protected herself against any man's
evil suggestions. But he, as the result showed, could not
have intercepted the opportunities for such suggestions.
Yet, why not? Was he not active? Was he not blooming? Blooming he was as Fanny herself.

Say, all our praises why should lords——?

Stop, that's not the line.

Say, all our roses why should girls engross?

The coachman showed rosy blossoms on his face deeper
even than his granddaughter's—*his* being drawn from the
ale cask, Fanny's from the fountains of the dawn. But,
in spite of his blooming face, some infirmities he had;
and one particularly in which he too much resembled a
crocodile. This lay in a monstrous inaptitude for turning
round. The crocodile, I presume, owes that inaptitude
to the absurd *length* of his back; but in our grandpapa it
arose rather from the absurd *breadth* of his back, combined, possibly, with some growing stiffness in his legs.
Now, upon this crocodile infirmity of his I planted a
human advantage for tendering my homage to Miss
Fanny. In defiance of all his honourable vigilance, no
sooner had he presented to us his mighty Jovian back
(what a field for displaying to mankind his royal scarlet!),
whilst inspecting professionally the buckles, the straps,
and the silvery turrets of his harness, than I raised Miss
Fanny's hand to my lips, and, by the mixed tenderness
and respectfulness of my manner, caused her easily to
understand how happy it would make me to rank upon
her list as No. 10 or 12, in which case a few casualties
amongst her lovers (and observe, they *hanged* liberally in
those days) might have promoted me speedily to the top
of the tree; as, on the other hand, with how much loyalty
of submission I acquiesced by anticipation in her award,
supposing that she should plant me in the very rear-ward
of her favour, as No. 199+1. Most truly I loved this
beautiful and ingenuous girl; and had it not been for the

Bath mail, timing all courtships by post-office allowance, heaven only knows what might have come of it. People talk of being over head and ears in love; now the mail was the cause that I sank only over ears in love, which, you know, still left a trifle of brain to overlook the whole conduct of the affair.

Ah, reader! when I look back upon those days, it seems to me that all things change—all things perish. 'Perish the roses and the palms of kings': perish even the crowns and trophies of Waterloo: thunder and lightning are not the thunder and lightning which I remember. Roses are degenerating. The Fannies of our island—though this I say with reluctance—are not visibly improving; and the Bath road is notoriously superannuated. Crocodiles, you will say, are stationary. Mr. Waterton tells me that the crocodile does *not* change; that a cayman, in fact, or an alligator, is just as good for riding upon as he was in the time of the Pharaohs. *That* may be; but the reason is, that the crocodile does not live fast—he is a slow coach. I believe it is generally understood among naturalists that the crocodile is a blockhead. It is my own impression that the Pharaohs were also blockheads. Now, as the Pharaohs and the crocodile domineered over Egyptian society, this accounts for a singular mistake that prevailed through innumerable generations on the Nile. The crocodile made the ridiculous blunder of supposing man to be meant chiefly for his own eating. Man, taking a different view of the subject, naturally met that mistake by another: he viewed the crocodile as a thing sometimes to worship, but always to run away from. And this continued until Mr. Waterton changed the relations between the animals. The mode of escaping from the reptile he showed to be, not by running away, but by leaping on its back, booted and spurred. The two animals had misunderstood each other. The use of the crocodile has now been cleared up—viz. to be ridden; and the Final Cause of Man is, that he may improve the health of the crocodile by riding him a fox-hunting before breakfast. And it is pretty certain that any crocodile, who has been regularly

hunted through the season, and is master of the weight
he carries, will take a six-barred gate now as well as ever
he would have done in the infancy of the pyramids.

If, therefore, the crocodile does *not* change, all things
else undeniably *do*: even the shadow of the pyramids
grows less. And often the restoration in vision of Fanny
and the Bath road makes me too pathetically sensible of
that truth. Out of the darkness, if I happen to call back
the image of Fanny, up rises suddenly from a gulf of
forty years a rose in June; or, if I think for an instant
of the rose in June, up rises the heavenly face of Fanny.
One after the other, like the antiphonies in the choral
service, rise Fanny and the rose in June, then back again
the rose in June and Fanny. Then come both together,
as in a chorus—roses and Fannies, Fannies and roses,
without end, thick as blossoms in paradise. Then comes
a venerable crocodile, in a royal livery of scarlet and gold,
with sixteen capes; and the crocodile is driving four-in-
hand from the box of the Bath mail. And suddenly we
upon the mail are pulled up by a mighty dial, sculptured
with the hours, that mingle with the heavens and the
heavenly host. Then all at once we are arrived at Marlborough forest, amongst the lovely households of the
roe-deer; the deer and their fawns retire into the dewy
thickets; the thickets are rich with roses; once again the
roses call up the sweet countenance of Fanny; and she,
being the granddaughter of a crocodile, awakens a dreadful host of semi-legendary animals—griffins, dragons,
basilisks, sphinxes—till at length the whole vision of
fighting images crowds into one towering armorial shield,
a vast emblazonry of human charities and human loveli-
ness that have perished, but quartered heraldically with
unutterable and demoniac natures, whilst over all rises,
as a surmounting crest, one fair female hand, with the
forefinger pointing, in sweet, sorrowful admonition, up-
wards to heaven, where is sculptured the eternal writing
which proclaims the frailty of earth and her children.

GOING DOWN WITH VICTORY

But the grandest chapter of our experience, within the whole mail-coach service, was on those occasions when we went down from London with the news of victory. A period of about ten years stretched from Trafalgar to Waterloo; the second and third years of which period (1806 and 1807) were comparatively sterile; but the other nine (from 1805 to 1815 inclusively) furnished a long succession of victories; the least of which, in such a contest of Titans, had an inappreciable value of position—partly for its absolute interference with the plans of our enemy, but still more from its keeping alive through central Europe the sense of a deep-seated vulnerability in France. Even to tease the coasts of our enemy, to mortify them by continual blockades, to insult them by capturing if it were but a baubling schooner under the eyes of their arrogant armies, repeated from time to time a sullen proclamation of power lodged in one quarter to which the hopes of Christendom turned in secret. How much more loudly must this proclamation have spoken in the audacity of having bearded the *élite* of their troops, and having beaten them in pitched battles! Five years of life it was worth paying down for the privilege of an outside place on a mail-coach, when carrying down the first tidings of any such event. And it is to be noted that, from our insular situation, and the multitude of our frigates disposable for the rapid transmission of intelligence, rarely did any unauthorized rumour steal away a prelibation from the first aroma of the regular dispatches. The government news was generally the earliest news.

From eight p.m., to fifteen or twenty minutes later, imagine the mails assembled on parade in Lombard Street, where, at that time, and not in St. Martin's-le-Grand, was seated the General Post Office. In what exact strength we mustered I do not remember; but, from the length of each separate *attelage*, we filled the street, though a long one, and though we were drawn up in

F 2

double file. On *any* night the spectacle was beautiful. The absolute perfection of all the appointments about the carriages and the harness, their strength, their brilliant cleanliness, their beautiful simplicity—but, more than all, the royal magnificence of the horses—were what might first have fixed the attention. Every carriage, on every morning in the year, was taken down to an official inspector for examination—wheels, axles, linchpins, pole, glasses, lamps, were all critically probed and tested. Every part of every carriage had been cleaned, every horse had been groomed, with as much rigour as if they belonged to a private gentleman; and that part of the spectacle offered itself always. But the night before us is a night of victory; and, behold! to the ordinary display, what a heart-shaking addition!—horses, men, carriages, all are dressed in laurels and flowers, oak-leaves and ribbons. The guards, as being officially his Majesty's servants, and of the coachmen such as are within the privilege of the post office, wear the royal liveries of course; and as it is summer (for all the *land* victories were naturally won in summer), they wear, on this fine evening, these liveries exposed to view, without any covering of upper coats. Such a costume, and the elaborate arrangement of the laurels in their hats, dilate their hearts, by giving to them openly a personal connexion with the great news, in which already they have the general interest of patriotism. That great national sentiment surmounts and quells all sense of ordinary distinctions. Those passengers who happen to be gentlemen are now hardly to be distinguished as such except by dress; for the usual reserve of their manner in speaking to the attendants has on this night melted away. One heart, one pride, one glory, connects every man by the transcendent bond of his national blood. The spectators, who are numerous beyond precedent, express their sympathy with these fervent feelings by continual hurrahs. Every moment are shouted aloud by the post-office servants, and summoned to draw up, the great ancestral names of cities known to history through a thousand years—Lincoln, Winchester, Portsmouth, Gloucester, Oxford, Bristol, Manchester, York, Newcastle, Edinburgh, Glasgow, Perth, Stirling, Aberdeen—expressing the grandeur of the empire by the antiquity of its towns, and the grandeur of the mail establishment by the diffusive radiation of its separate missions. Every moment you hear the thunder of lids locked down upon the mail-bags. That sound to each individual mail is the signal for drawing off, which process is the finest part of the entire spectacle. Then come the horses into play. Horses! can these be horses that bound off with the action and gestures of leopards? What stir!—what sea-like ferment! —what a thundering of wheels!—what a trampling of hoofs!—what a sounding of trumpets!—what farewell cheers—what redoubling peals of brotherly congratulation, connecting the name of the particular mail—'Liverpool for ever!'—with the name of the particular victory —'Badajoz for ever!' or 'Salamanca for ever!' The half-slumbering consciousness, that all night long and all the next day—perhaps for even a longer period—many of these mails, like fire racing along a train of gunpowder, will be kindling at every instant new successions of burning joy, has an obscure effect of multiplying the victory itself, by multiplying to the imagination into infinity the stages of its progressive diffusion. A fiery arrow seems to be let loose, which from that moment is destined to travel, without intermission, westwards for three hundred miles—northwards for six hundred; and the sympathy of our Lombard Street friends at parting is exalted a hundredfold by a sort of visionary sympathy with the yet slumbering sympathies which in so vast a succession we are going to awake.

Liberated from the embarrassments of the city, and issuing into the broad uncrowded avenues of the northern suburbs, we soon begin to enter upon our natural pace of ten miles an hour. In the broad light of the summer evening, the sun, perhaps, only just at the point of setting, we are seen from every story of every house. Heads of every age crowd to the windows—young and old

understand the language of our victorious symbols—and
rolling volleys of sympathizing cheers run along us, behind us, and before us. The beggar, rearing himself
against the wall, forgets his lameness—real or assumed—
thinks not of his whining trade, but stands erect, with
bold exulting smiles, as we pass him. The victory has
healed him, and says, Be thou whole! Women and
children, from garrets alike and cellars, through infinite
London, look down or look up with loving eyes upon
our gay ribbons and our martial laurels; sometimes kiss
their hands; sometimes hang out, as signals of affection,
pocket-handkerchiefs, aprons, dusters, anything that, by
catching the summer breezes, will express an aerial jubila-
tion. On the London side of Barnet, to which we draw
near within a few minutes after nine, observe that private
carriage which is approaching us. The weather being so
warm, the glasses are all down; and one may read, as on
the stage of a theatre, everything that goes on within.
It contains three ladies—one likely to be 'mamma', and
two of seventeen or eighteen, who are probably her
daughters. What lovely animation, what beautiful un-
premeditated pantomime, explaining to us every syllable
that passes, in these ingenuous girls! By the sudden start
and raising of the hands, on first discovering our laurelled
equipage!—by the sudden movement and appeal to the
elder lady from both of them—and by the heightened
colour on their animated countenances, we can almost
hear them saying, 'See, see! Look at their laurels! Oh,
mamma! there has been a great battle in Spain; and it
has been a great victory.' In a moment we are on the
point of passing them. We passengers—I on the box, and
the two on the roof behind me—raise our hats to the
ladies; the coachman makes his professional salute with
the whip; the guard even, though punctilious on the
matter of his dignity as an officer under the Crown,
touches his hat. The ladies move to us, in return, with
a winning graciousness of gesture; all smile on each side
in a way that nobody could misunderstand, and that
nothing short of a grand national sympathy could so

instantaneously prompt. Will these ladies say that we
are nothing to *them*? Oh, no; they will not say *that*.
They cannot deny—they do not deny—that for this night
they are our sisters; gentle or simple, scholar or illiterate
servant, for twelve hours to come, we on the outside have
the honour to be their brothers. Those poor women,
again, who stop to gaze upon us with delight at the
entrance of Barnet, and seem, by their air of weariness,
to be returning from labour—do you mean to say that
they are washerwomen and charwomen? Oh, my poor
friend, you are quite mistaken. I assure you they stand
in a far higher rank; for this one night they feel themselves by birthright to be daughters of England, and
answer to no humbler title.

Every joy, however, even rapturous joy—such is the
sad law of earth—may carry with it grief, or fear of grief,
to some. Three miles beyond Barnet, we see approaching
us another private carriage, nearly repeating the circumstances of the former case. Here, also, the glasses are all
down—here, also, is an elderly lady seated; but the two
daughters are missing; for the single young person sitting
by the lady's side seems to be an attendant—so I judge
from her dress, and her air of respectful reserve. The lady
is in mourning; and her countenance expresses sorrow.
At first she does not look up; so that I believe she is
not aware of our approach, until she hears the measured
beating of our horses' hoofs. Then she raises her eyes
to settle them painfully on our triumphal equipage. Our
decorations explain the case to her at once; but she be-
holds them with apparent anxiety, or even with terror.
Some time before this, I, finding it difficult to hit a flying
mark, when embarrassed by the coachman's person and
reins intervening, had given to the guard a *Courier* evening paper, containing the 'Gazette', for the next carriage
that might pass. Accordingly he tossed it in, so folded
that the huge capitals expressing some such legend as
GLORIOUS VICTORY might catch the eye at once. To see
the paper, however, at all, interpreted as it was by our
ensigns of triumph, explained everything; and, if the

guard were right in thinking the lady to have received it
with a gesture of horror, it could not be doubtful that she
had suffered some deep personal affliction in connexion
with this Spanish war.

Here, now, was the case of one who, having formerly
suffered, might, erroneously perhaps, be distressing herself with anticipations of another similar suffering. That
same night, and hardly three hours later, occurred the
reverse case. A poor woman, who too probably would
find herself, in a day or two, to have suffered the heaviest
of afflictions by the battle, blindly allowed herself to
express an exultation so unmeasured in the news and its
details as gave to her the appearance which amongst
Celtic Highlanders is called *fey*. This was at some little
town where we changed horses an hour or two after midnight. Some fair or wake had kept the people up out of
their beds, and had occasioned a partial illumination of
the stalls and booths, presenting an unusual but very
impressive effect. We saw many lights moving about as
we drew near; and perhaps the most striking scene on
the whole route was our reception at this place. The
flashing of torches and the beautiful radiance of blue
lights (technically, Bengal lights) upon the heads of our
horses; the fine effect of such a showery and ghostly illumination falling upon our flowers and glittering laurels;
whilst all around ourselves, that formed a centre of light,
the darkness gathered on the rear and flanks in massy
blackness; these optical splendours, together with the
prodigious enthusiasm of the people, composed a picture
at once scenical and affecting, theatrical and holy. As
we stayed for three or four minutes, I alighted; and immediately from a dismantled stall in the street, where no
doubt she had been presiding through the earlier part of
the night, advanced eagerly a middle-aged woman. The
sight of my newspaper it was that had drawn her attention upon myself. The victory which we were carrying
down to the provinces on *this* occasion was the imperfect
one of Talavera—imperfect for its results, such was the
virtual treachery of the Spanish general, Cuesta, but not

imperfect in its ever-memorable heroism. I told her the
main outline of the battle. The agitation of her enthusiasm had been so conspicuous when listening, and when
first applying for information, that I could not but ask
her if she had not some relative in the Peninsular army.
Oh, yes; her only son was there. In what regiment? He
was a trooper in the 23rd Dragoons. My heart sank
within me as she made that answer. This sublime regiment, which an Englishman should never mention without raising his hat to their memory, had made the most
memorable and effective charge recorded in military
annals. They leaped their horses—*over* a trench where
they could, *into* it, and with the result of death or mutila-
tion, when they could *not*. What proportion cleared the
trench is nowhere stated. Those who *did*, closed up and
went down upon the enemy with such divinity of fervour
(I use the word *divinity* by design: the inspiration of
God must have prompted this movement to those whom
even then He was calling to His presence), that two results
followed. As regarded the enemy, this 23rd Dragoons,
not, I believe, originally three hundred and fifty strong,
paralysed a French column, six thousand strong, then
ascended the hill, and fixed the gaze of the whole French
army. As regarded themselves, the 23rd were supposed
at first to have been barely not annihilated; but eventu-
ally, I believe, about one in four survived. And this,
then, was the regiment—a regiment already for some
hours glorified and hallowed to the ear of all London, as
lying stretched, by a large majority, upon one bloody
aceldama—in which the young trooper served whose
mother was now talking in a spirit of such joyous enthusiasm. Did I tell her the truth? Had I the heart to break
up her dreams? No. To-morrow, said I to myself—to-
morrow, or the next day, will publish the worst. For one
night more, wherefore should she not sleep in peace?
After to-morrow the chances are too many that peace
will forsake her pillow. This brief respite, then, let her
owe to *my* gift and *my* forbearance. But, if I told her
not of the bloody price that had been paid, not, therefore,

was I silent on the contributions from her son's regiment to that day's service and glory. I showed her not the funeral banners under which the noble regiment was sleeping. I lifted not the overshadowing laurels from the bloody trench in which horse and rider lay mangled together. But I told her how these dear children of England, officers and privates, had leaped their horses over all obstacles as gaily as hunters to the morning's chase. I told her how they rode their horses into the mists of death (saying to myself, but not saying to *her*—and laid down their young lives for thee, O mother England! as willingly, poured out their noble blood as cheerfully, as ever, after a long day's sport, when infants, they had rested their wearied heads upon their mother's knees, or had sunk to sleep in her arms). Strange it is, yet true, that she seemed to have no fears for her son's safety, even after this knowledge that the 23rd Dragoons had been memorably engaged; but so much was she enraptured by the knowledge that *his* regiment, and therefore that *he*, had rendered conspicuous service in the dreadful conflict—a service which had actually made them, within the last twelve hours, the foremost topic of conversation in London—so absolutely was fear swallowed up in joy—that, in the mere simplicity of her fervent nature, the poor woman threw her arms round my neck, as she thought of her son, and gave to *me* the kiss which secretly was meant for *him*.

JAMES HENRY LEIGH HUNT

ON GETTING UP ON COLD MORNINGS

An Italian author—Giulio Cordara, a Jesuit—has written a poem upon insects, which he begins by insisting that those troublesome and abominable little animals were created for our annoyance, and that they were certainly not inhabitants of Paradise. We of the north may dispute this piece of theology; but on the other hand it is as clear as the snow on the house-tops that Adam was not under the necessity of shaving; and that when Eve walked out of her delicious bower she did not step upon ice three inches thick.

Some people say it is a very easy thing to get up of a cold morning. You have only, they tell you, to take the resolution; and the thing is done. This may be very true; just as a boy at school has only to take a flogging, and the thing is over. But we have not at all made up our minds upon it; and we find it a very pleasant exercise to discuss the matter, candidly, before we get up. This, at least, is not idling, though it may be lying. It affords an excellent answer to those who ask how lying in bed can be indulged in by a reasoning being—a rational creature. How? Why, with the argument calmly at work in one's head, and the clothes over one's shoulder. Oh—it is a fine way of spending a sensible, impartial half-hour.

If these people would be more charitable they would get on with their argument better. But they are apt to reason so ill, and to assert so dogmatically, that one could wish to have them round one's bed, of a bitter morning, and *lie* before their faces. They ought to hear both sides of the bed, the inside and out. If they cannot entertain themselves with their own thoughts for half an hour or so, it is not the fault of those who can.

Candid inquiries into one's decumbency, besides the greater or less privileges to be allowed a man in proportion to his ability of keeping early hours, the work given his faculties, &c., will at least concede their due merits to such representations as the following. In the first place, says the injured but calm appealer, I have been warm all night, and find my system in a state perfectly suitable to a warm-blooded animal. To get out of this state into the cold, besides the inharmonious and uncritical abruptness of the transition, is so unnatural to such a creature, that the poets, refining upon the tortures of the damned, make one of their greatest agonies consist in being suddenly transported from heat to cold—from fire to ice. They are 'haled' out of their 'beds', says Milton, by 'harpy-footed furies'—fellows who come to call them. On my first movement towards the anticipation of getting up I find that such parts of the sheets and bolster as are exposed to the air of the room are stone-cold. On opening my eyes, the first thing that meets them is my own breath rolling forth, as if in the open air, like smoke out of a chimney. Think of this symptom. Then I turn my eyes sideways and see the window all frozen over. Think of that. Then the servant comes in. 'It is very cold this morning, is it not?'—'Very cold, sir.'—'Very cold indeed, isn't it?'—'Very cold indeed, sir.'— 'More than usually so, isn't it, even for this weather?' (Here the servant's wit and good-nature are put to a considerable test, and the inquirer lies on thorns for the answer.) 'Why, sir . . . I think it *is*.' (Good creature! There is not a better or more truth-telling servant going.) 'I must rise, however—get me some warm water.' Here comes a fine interval between the departure of the servant and the arrival of the hot water; during which, of course, it is of 'no use' to get up. The hot water comes. 'Is it quite hot?'—'Yes, sir.'—'Perhaps too hot for shaving; I must wait a little?'—'No, sir; it will just do.' (There is an over-nice propriety sometimes, an officious zeal of virtue, a little troublesome.) 'Oh—the shirt—you must air my clean shirt; linen gets very damp this weather.'—'Yes, sir.' Here another delicious five minutes. A knock at the door. 'Oh, the shirt—very well. My stockings—I think the stockings had better be aired too.'—'Very well, sir.' Here another interval. At length everything is ready, except myself. I now, continues our incumbent (a happy word, by the by, for a country vicar)—I now cannot help thinking a good deal—who can?—upon the unnecessary and villainous custom of shaving: it is a thing so unmanly (here I nestle closer)—so effeminate (here I recoil from an unlucky step into the colder part of the bed). No wonder that the Queen of France took part with the rebels against that degenerate king, her husband, who first affronted her smooth visage with a face like her own. The Emperor Julian never showed the luxuriancy of his genius to better advantage than in reviving the flowing beard. Look at Cardinal Bembo's picture—at Michaelangelo's —at Titian's—at Shakespeare's—at Fletcher's—at Spenser's—at Chaucer's—at Alfred's—at Plato's—I could name a great man for every tick of my watch. Look at the Turks, a grave and otiose people. Think of Haroun Al Raschid and Bedreddin Hassan. Think of Wortley Montagu, the worthy son of his mother, above the prejudice of his time. Look at the Persian gentlemen, whom one is ashamed of meeting about the suburbs, their dress and appearance are so much finer than our own. Lastly, think of the razor itself—how totally opposed to every sensation of bed—how cold, how edgy, how hard! how utterly different from anything like the warm and circling amplitude, which

> Sweetly recommends itself
> Unto our gentle senses.

Add to this—benumbed fingers, which may help you to cut yourself, a quivering body, a frozen towel, and a ewer full of ice; and he that says there is nothing to oppose in all this, only shows that he has no merit in opposing it.

Thomson the poet, who exclaims in his *Seasons*—

> Falsely luxurious! Will not man awake?

used to lie in bed till noon, because he said he had no motive in getting up. He could imagine the good of rising; but then he could also imagine the good of lying still; and his exclamation, it must be allowed, was made upon the summer-time, not winter. We must proportion the argument to the individual character. A money-getter may be drawn out of his bed by three or four pence; but this will not suffice for a student. A proud man may say, 'What shall I think of myself, if I don't get up?' but the more humble one will be content to waive this prodigious notion of himself, out of respect to his kindly bed. The mechanical man shall get up without any ado at all; and so shall the barometer. An ingenious lier in bed will find hard matter of discussion even on the score of health and longevity. He will ask us for our proofs and precedents of the ill effects of lying later in cold weather; and sophisticate much on the advantages of an even temperature of body; of the natural propensity (pretty universal) to have one's way; and of the animals that roll themselves up and sleep all the winter. As to longevity, he will ask whether the longest is of necessity the best; and whether Holborn is the handsomest street in London.

WALTER BAGEHOT

BOSCASTLE

WHATEVER doubt there may be as to the truth of Mr. Darwin's speculations on other points, there is no doubt that they are applicable to the coast cliffs of north Cornwall. No doubt every cliff owes its being to natural selection. All the weak rocks have been worn away by ages of conflict with the whole Atlantic, and only the strong rocks are left. They often are worn, too, into shapes resembling the spare and gigantic veterans of many wars; wherever the subtle ocean detected a bit of soft stone, it set to and wore it away, so that the grim masses which stand are all granite—the 'bones and sinews' of geology. The peculiarity of the coast, among other beautiful ones, is that it is a mere coast; the picturesque stops at the cliff line. In the adjacent coast of north and west the high hills of the interior send down many streams, which in the course of ages have hollowed out deep valleys and softened with woody banks the wild and stony fields. But Cornwall is a thin county, has no deep interior to be a source of big streams, and the little ones which trickle forth have to rush over a rock too hard and too bleak for them to wear it into delicate valleys. But the shore line is charming, not only because the waves swell with the force of the full ocean, while the bays are scooped and the rocks scarred by its incessant hand—its careful hand, I had almost said, so minute and pervading are its touches— but the hard grey rock of the shore also contributes much to make *clean foam*. The softer rocks always mix something of their own alloy with the pure sea, but the grey grit here has no discolouring power; the white line of spray dances from headland to headland as pure and crystal-like as if it had not touched the earth.

But I have no intention of wearying you with a description of scenery. The seashore is a pretty thing, but it is not a discovery of my own. The coast is very curious—I do not mean in those ante-Roman remains which your most learned contributor has so well described. I cannot presume to tell you whether in truth in this place, as in so many others, according to the last ideas and perhaps the hardest terms of ethnology, the dolichocephalic race of men attacked and extirpated the brachycephalic, or short-headed, ten thousand years before history began. Anyhow, if the theory is true, it must have been cold work on these cliffs and moors, when you picked up mussels and (if possible) cray-fish, and cut skins, if you had any, into clothes with a blunt flint, when fire had just come in as a new and (Conservative thought!) suspicious thing, and tattooing was still the best of the fine arts. The year A.D. 1866 has defects, but it is better certainly than the B.C. 18,660, if the human races were really about then. But, as I said, I cannot deal with such matters; I have only a little to say about the changes of life and civilization which this coast marks in the last century or two.

We are familiar with the present state of trade, and with the phenomena it creates and the conditions it requires. It shows itself to the eye at once in immense warehouses, cities spreading over miles and miles, and not seeming even to anticipate a boundary, a population daily streaming from the thinly inhabited outskirts, and daily concentrating itself more and more in the already thronged cities. Commerce gives much to those who have much, and from such as have little it takes that little away. But the pre-requisites of our commerce are of recent growth, and our ancestors even lately did not possess them. They are—large and ready capital, rapid and cheap land-carriage, the power of making great breakwaters to keep out storms, the power of making large docks to hold many vessels, the ability to protect and the confidence to amass great wealth close to the sea-shore. But a very few generations ago these gifts were wanting. It was useless to bring all merchandise to one port, for when there you could not use it; no railway and

no canal distributed bulky articles; they had to be
brought by water to the nearest possible market; they
might nearly as well have stayed where they were grown,
if they had to be conveyed a hundred or two hundred
miles when here. All our great protective works against
the sea, all our great accumulative works at the
great ports, are modern in the strictest sense, post-
modern, as geologists would say, part of the 'drift' of
this age.

But though in theory we know these things, yet they
come upon us with a sudden completeness when we see
the sort of place our ancestors thought a port. Boscastle
is as good an example of their idea as can be found. It
is a creek shaped like a capital S, with, I should think, the
earliest and smallest breakwater on record just about the
middle. The sea runs with great violence on all this coast,
and no open bay is safe for a moment. But the turn or
crook of the Boscastle creek, which I have endeavoured to
describe by likening it to the letter S, in a great measure
protects it, and even early masons were able to run out on
the solid rock some few feet of compact stones, which help
to add to the shelter. The whole creek is never nearly as
broad as Regent Street, and it gradually runs away to be
narrower than the Strand, while at the point of the breakwater there is a real Temple Bar, which hardly seems wide
enough for a ship at all. The whole thing, when you first
look down on it, gives you the notion that you are looking
at a big port through a diminishing glass, so complete is
the whole equipment, and yet so absurdly disproportion-
ate, according to our notions, is the size. The principal
harbour of Lilliput probably had just this look. But
though its size across is small, the rocks which make its
jaws are very formidable, and the sea foams against them
in an unpleasant manner. I suppose we ought to think
much of the courage with which sailors face such dangers,
and of the feelings of their wives and families when they
wait the return of their husbands and fathers; but my
City associations at once carried me away to the poor
underwriter who should insure against loss at such a place.

3817   G

How he would murmur, 'Oh! my premium,' as he saw the ship tossing up to the great black rock and the ugly breakwater, and seeming likely enough to hit both. I shall not ask at Lloyd's what is the rate for Boscastle rocks, for I remember the grave rebuke I once got from a serious underwriter when I said some other such place was pretty. 'Pretty! I should think it was,' he answered; 'why it is lined with our money!'

But our ancestors had no choice but to use such places. They could not make London and Liverpool; they had not the money; what wealth existed was scattered all over the country; the central money-market was not. There was no use in going to the goldsmiths who made Lombard Street to ask for a couple of millions to make docks or breakwaters, even if our science could have then made large specimens of the latter, which it could not. And, as I said before, these large emporia when made would have been quite useless; the auxiliary facilities which alone make such places serviceable did not exist. The neighbourhoods of Bideford and Boscastle had then to trust to Bideford and Boscastle; they had no access to London or Liverpool; they relied on their local port, and if that failed them had no resource or substitute.

The fringe of petty ports all over our coasts serves to explain the multitudes of old country houses, in proportion to the populations of old times, which are mouldering in out-of-the-way and often very ugly places. The tourist thinks—how did people come to build in such an inaccessible and unpicturesque place? But few of our old gentry cared for what we now call the beauties of nature; they built on their own estates when they could, and if those estates were near some wretched little haven they were much pleased. The sea was the railway of those days; it brought, as it did to Ellangowan in Dirk Hatterack's time, brandy for the men and 'pinners' for the women to the lonest of coast castles. According to popular belief, King Arthur himself thus lived. The famous castle of Tintagel hangs over the edge of a cliff,

right over the next little bay to that of Boscastle—a very
lone place, where a boat could get out to sea if the pilot
knew the place, but where no stranger or pirate could get
in with the tiniest craft, under peril of his life. By land,
too, the Saxon must have had many a weary mile of bog
and moorland to cross before he reached the crag's edge,
and had very tough walls to deal with there, for they have
not been repaired these thousand years, and at perhaps
the most windy point in England some of them are
standing still. King Arthur is out of luck just now. The
sceptical, prosaic historians disbelieve in him, and the
ethnologists despise him. What indeed is the interest of a
dubious antiquity of thirteen hundred years, if we really
can get to the people who dwelt 'near Bedford' side by
side in daily life with the long-horned rhinoceros and the
woolly-haired mammoth? So between the *literati* who
think him too far off to believe in, and the *literati* who
consider him too modern to take an interest in, King
Arthur is at his nadir. But how singular was his zenith
before! Whatever may be the doubt as to the existence of
his person, there is no doubt as to the existence of his
reputation, and it is the queerest perhaps even in legend.
If he was anything, he was a Celt who resisted the
Teutonic invaders, and yet years after, when these very
Teutons created their own chivalry, they made into a
fancied model of it this Celt, who never dreamed of it,
who could not have understood an iota of it, who hated
and perhaps slew the ancestors of those who made
it. There are hundreds of kings whose reality is as
uncertain as Arthur's, and some, though not many, whose
fame has been as great as his; but there is no king or hero
perhaps whose reality, if it were proved, *must* be so
inconsistent with his fame.

I did not intend to have gone into this matter, but the
strong legend of the place was too much for me. I
meant only to have said that it was in the ruined small
ports and coast granges and castles of Queen Elizabeth's
time that our Raleighs, and Drakes, and Frobishers were
formed. In the ante-Lancashire period, now forgotten,

Devon was a great mercantile county, and adjacent Cornwall shared, though somewhat less, in its power and its celebrity. It was 'Devonshire', local enthusiasts have said, 'which beat the Spanish Armada.' I am not sure of the history; according to my memory, the Armada was beaten by the waves; but Devonshire is right in this—she bred a main part of those who would have resisted the Armada, and who in that age fought the Spaniards whenever, in either hemisphere, propitious fate sent an opportunity.

Mr. Arnold has lately been writing on the influence of the Celtic character on the English. I wish he would consider whether the predominance of Southern England in old times, say in the Tudor period, had nothing to do with the largely romantic elements in the characters of those times. 'North of the Trent' the population was always thin till the manufacturing times, and there must have been a much scantier subjacent race of Celts there than in Devon and the South. It may be accident, but certainly the Tudor Englishman tends to crop up hereabouts. There is Mr. Kingsley, who was born, I believe, at Clovelly, and has drunk into his very nature all the life of this noble coast. There is in his style a vigour, softened, yet unrelaxed, which is like the spirit of these places. If he is not more like a Tudor Englishman than a nineteenth-century Englishman, then words have no meaning, and Mr. Arnold may be able to prove, though I can but suggest, that the source of all this compacted energy, fancy, and unsoundness lies in the universal local predominance of the Celtic nature. The datum is certain at least; we can all see that Mr. Kingsley is not like the pure Goth of Lancashire, for there can be little of the Celt there.

I do not feel able to confirm these ethnological speculations by any personal observations of my own upon the Boscastle natives. Their principal feature, to a stranger at least, is a theory they have that their peculiar pronunciation of the English language is the most correct. I asked a native the way to the chemist's, pronouncing *ch*,

as is usual, like a *k*. The man looked at me wondering;
then I repeated—when he said with pity, 'You mean the
*tch*emist's'. Is this the last soft remnant of a Celtic gut-
tural, or only the outcome of the inbred pragmaticalness
of the natural rural mind?

ROBERT LOUIS STEVENSON

WALKING TOURS

It must not be imagined that a walking tour, as some
would have us fancy, is merely a better or worse way of
seeing the country. There are many ways of seeing landscape quite as good; and none more vivid, in spite of
canting dilettantes, than from a railway train. But landscape on a walking tour is quite accessory. He who is
indeed of the brotherhood does not voyage in quest of
the picturesque, but of certain jolly humours—of the
hope and spirit with which the march begins at morning,
and the peace and spiritual repletion of the evening's rest.
He cannot tell whether he puts his knapsack on, or takes
it off, with more delight. The excitement of the departure
puts him in key for that of the arrival. Whatever he
does is not only a reward in itself, but will be further
rewarded in the sequel; and so pleasure leads on to
pleasure in an endless chain. It is this that so few can
understand; they will either be always lounging or always
at five miles an hour; they do not play off the one against
the other, prepare all day for the evening, and all evening
for the next day. And, above all, it is here that your
overwalker fails of comprehension. His heart rises against
those who drink their curaçao in liqueur glasses, when
he himself can swill it in a brown john. He will not
believe that the flavour is more delicate in the smaller
dose. He will not believe that to walk this unconscionable
distance is merely to stupefy and brutalize himself, and
come to his inn, at night, with a sort of frost on his five
wits, and a starless night of darkness in his spirit. Not
for him the mild luminous evening of the temperate
walker! He has nothing left of man but a physical need
for bedtime and a double nightcap; and even his pipe,
if he be a smoker, will be savourless and disenchanted.
It is the fate of such a one to take twice as much trouble
as is needed to obtain happiness, and miss the happiness

in the end; he is the man of the proverb, in short, who goes farther and fares worse.

Now, to be properly enjoyed, a walking tour should be gone upon alone. If you go in a company, or even in pairs, it is no longer a walking tour in anything but name; it is something else and more in the nature of a picnic. A walking tour should be gone upon alone, because freedom is of the essence; because you should be able to stop and go on, and follow this way or that, as the freak takes you; and because you must have your own pace, and neither trot alongside a champion walker, nor mince in time with a girl. And then you must be open to all impressions and let your thoughts take colour from what you see. You should be as a pipe for any wind to play upon. 'I cannot see the wit,' says Hazlitt, 'of walking and talking at the same time. When I am in the country, I wish to vegetate like the country,' which is the gist of all that can be said upon the matter. There should be no cackle of voices at your elbow, to jar on the meditative silence of the morning. And so long as a man is reasoning he cannot surrender himself to that fine intoxication that comes of much motion in the open air, that begins in a sort of dazzle and sluggishness of the brain, and ends in a peace that passes comprehension.

During the first day or so of any tour there are moments of bitterness, when the traveller feels more than coldly towards his knapsack, when he is half in a mind to throw it bodily over the hedge and, like Christian on a similar occasion, 'give three leaps and go on singing'. And yet it soon acquires a property of easiness. It becomes magnetic; the spirit of the journey enters into it. And no sooner have you passed the straps over your shoulder than the lees of sleep are cleared from you, you pull yourself together with a shake, and fall at once into your stride. And surely, of all possible moods, this, in which a man takes the road, is the best. Of course, if he *will* keep thinking of his anxieties, if he *will* open the merchant Abudah's chest and walk arm in arm with the hag

—why, wherever he is, and whether he walk fast or slow, the chances are that he will not be happy. And so much the more shame to himself! There are perhaps thirty men setting forth at that same hour, and I would lay a large wager there is not another dull face among the thirty. It would be a fine thing to follow, in a coat of darkness, one after another of these wayfarers, some summer morning, for the first few miles upon the road. This one, who walks fast, with a keen look in his eyes, is all concentrated in his own mind; he is up at his loom, weaving and weaving, to set the landscape to words. This one peers about, as he goes, among the grasses; he waits by the canal to watch the dragon-flies; he leans on the gate of the pasture, and cannot look enough upon the complacent kine. And here comes another talking, laughing, and gesticulating to himself. His face changes from time to time, as indignation flashes from his eyes or anger clouds his forehead. He is composing articles, delivering orations, and conducting the most impassioned interviews, by the way. A little farther on, and it is as like as not he will begin to sing. And well for him, supposing him to be no great master in that art, if he stumble across no stolid peasant at a corner; for on such an occasion, I scarcely know which is the more troubled, or whether it is worse to suffer the confusion of your troubadour or the unfeigned alarm of your clown. A sedentary population, accustomed, besides, to the strange mechanical bearing of the common tramp, can in no wise explain to itself the gaiety of these passers-by. I knew one man who was arrested as a runaway lunatic, because, although a full-grown person with a red beard, he skipped as he went like a child. And you would be astonished if I were to tell you all the grave and learned heads who have confessed to me that, when on walking tours, they sang— and sang very ill—and had a pair of red ears when, as described above, the inauspicious peasant plumped into their arms from round a corner. And here, lest you should think I am exaggerating, is Hazlitt's own confession, from his essay *On going a Journey*, which is so

good that there should be a tax levied on all who have
not read it:

'Give me the clear blue sky over my head,' says he,
'and the green turf beneath my feet, a winding road
before me, and a three hours' march to dinner—and then
to thinking! It is hard if I cannot start some game on
these lone heaths. I laugh, I run, I leap, I sing for joy.'

Bravo! After that adventure of my friend with the
policeman, you would not have cared, would you, to publish that in the first person? But we have no bravery
nowadays, and, even in books, must all pretend to be as
dull and foolish as our neighbours. It was not so with
Hazlitt. And notice how learned he is (as, indeed,
throughout the essay) in the theory of walking tours. He
is none of your athletic men in purple stockings, who
walk their fifty miles a day: three hours' march is
his ideal. And then he must have a winding road, the
epicure!

Yet there is one thing I object to in these words of
his, one thing in the great master's practice that seems
to me not wholly wise. I do not approve of that leaping
and running. Both of these hurry the respiration; they
both shake up the brain out of its glorious open-air confusion; and they both break the pace. Uneven walking
is not so agreeable to the body, and it distracts and
irritates the mind. Whereas, when once you have fallen
into an equable stride, it requires no conscious thought
from you to keep it up, and yet it prevents you from
thinking earnestly of anything else. Like knitting, like
the work of a copying clerk, it gradually neutralizes and
sets to sleep the serious activity of the mind. We can
think of this or that, lightly and laughingly, as a child
thinks, or as we think in a morning doze; we can make
puns or puzzle out acrostics, and trifle in a thousand ways
with words and rhymes; but when it comes to honest
work, when we come to gather ourselves together for an
effort, we may sound the trumpet as loud and long as
we please; the great barons of the mind will not rally
to the standard, but sit, each one, at home, warming his

hands over his own fire and brooding on his own private thought!

In the course of a day's walk, you see, there is much variance in the mood. From the exhilaration of the start, to the happy phlegm of the arrival, the change is certainly great. As the day goes on, the traveller moves from the one extreme towards the other. He becomes more and more incorporated with the material landscape, and the open-air drunkenness grows upon him with great strides, until he posts along the road, and sees everything about him, as in a cheerful dream. The first is certainly brighter, but the second stage is the more peaceful. A man does not make so many articles towards the end, nor does he laugh aloud; but the purely animal pleasures, the sense of physical well-being, the delight of every inhalation, of every time the muscles tighten down the thigh, console him for the absence of the others, and bring him to his destination still content.

Nor must I forget to say a word on bivouacs. You come to a milestone on a hill, or some place where deep ways meet under trees; and off goes the knapsack, and down you sit to smoke a pipe in the shade. You sink into yourself, and the birds come round and look at you, and your smoke dissipates upon the afternoon under the blue dome of heaven; and the sun lies warm upon your feet, and the cool air visits your neck and turns aside your open shirt. If you are not happy, you must have an evil conscience. You may dally as long as you like by the roadside. It is almost as if the millennium were arrived, when we shall throw our clocks and watches over the house-top, and remember time and seasons no more. Not to keep hours for a lifetime is, I was going to say, to live for ever. You have no idea, unless you have tried it, how endlessly long is a summer's day, that you measure out only by hunger, and bring to an end only when you are drowsy. I know a village where there are hardly any clocks, where no one knows more of the days of the week than by a sort of instinct for the fête on Sundays, and where only one person can tell you the day of the month,

and she is generally wrong; and if people were aware how
slow Time journeyed in that village, and what armfuls
of spare hours he gives, over and above the bargain, to
its wise inhabitants, I believe there would be a stampede
out of London, Liverpool, Paris, and a variety of large
towns, where the clocks lose their heads, and shake the
hours out each one faster than the other, as though they
were all in a wager. And all these foolish pilgrims would
each bring his own misery along with him, in a watch-
pocket! It is to be noticed, there were no clocks and
watches in the much-vaunted days before the flood. It
follows, of course, there were no appointments, and
punctuality was not yet thought upon. 'Though ye take
from a covetous man all his treasure,' says Milton, 'he
has yet one jewel left; ye cannot deprive him of his
covetousness.' And so I would say of a modern man of
business, you may do what you will for him, put him in
Eden, give him the elixir of life—he has still a flaw at
heart, he still has his business habits. Now, there is no
time when business habits are more mitigated than on
a walking tour. And so during these halts, as I say, you
will feel almost free.

But it is at night, and after dinner, that the best hour
comes. There are no such pipes to be smoked as those
that follow a good day's march; the flavour of the
tobacco is a thing to be remembered, it is so dry and
aromatic, so full and so fine. If you wind up the evening
with grog, you will own there was never such grog; at
every sip a jocund tranquillity spreads about your limbs,
and sits easily in your heart. If you read a book—and
you will never do so save by fits and starts—you find
the language strangely racy and harmonious; words take
a new meaning; single sentences possess the ear for half
an hour together; and the writer endears himself to you,
at every page, by the nicest coincidence of sentiment.
It seems as if it were a book you had written yourself in
a dream. To all we have read on such occasions we look
back with special favour. 'It was on the 10th of April
1798,' says Hazlitt, with amorous precision, 'that I sat

down to a volume of the *New Heloïse*, at the Inn at
Llangollen, over a bottle of sherry and a cold chicken.'
I should wish to quote more, for though we are mighty
fine fellows nowadays, we cannot write like Hazlitt. And,
talking of that, a volume of Hazlitt's essays would be
a capital pocket-book on such a journey; so would a
volume of Heine's songs; and for *Tristram Shandy* I can
pledge a fair experience.

If the evening be fine and warm, there is nothing better
in life than to lounge before the inn door in the sunset,
or lean over the parapet of the bridge, to watch the weeds
and the quick fishes. It is then, if ever, that you taste
joviality to the full significance of that audacious word.
Your muscles are so agreeably slack, you feel so clean
and so strong and so idle, that whether you move or sit
still, whatever you do is done with pride and a kingly
sort of pleasure. You fall in talk with any one, wise or
foolish, drunk or sober. And it seems as if a hot walk
purged you, more than of anything else, of all narrowness
and pride, and left curiosity to play its part freely, as
in a child or a man of science. You lay aside all your
own hobbies, to watch provincial humours develop themselves before you, now as a laughable farce, and now
grave and beautiful like an old tale.

Or perhaps you are left to your own company for the
night, and surly weather imprisons you by the fire. You
may remember how Burns, numbering past pleasures,
dwells upon the hours when he has been 'happy thinking'. It is a phrase that may well perplex a poor modern
girt about on every side by clocks and chimes, and
haunted, even at night, by flaming dial-plates. For we
are all so busy, and have so many far-off projects to
realize, and castles in the fire to turn into solid, habitable
mansions on a gravel soil, that we can find no time for
pleasure trips into the Land of Thought and among the
Hills of Vanity. Changed times, indeed, when we must
sit all night, beside the fire, with folded hands; and a
changed world for most of us, when we find we can pass
the hours without discontent, and be happy thinking.

We are in such haste to be doing, to be writing, to be
gathering gear, to make our voice audible a moment in
the derisive silence of eternity, that we forget that one
thing, of which these are but the parts—namely, to live.
We fall in love, we drink hard, we run to and fro upon
the earth like frightened sheep. And now you are to ask
yourself if, when all is done, you would not have been
better to sit by the fire at home, and be happy thinking.
To sit still and contemplate—to remember the faces of
women without desire, to be pleased by the great deeds
of men without envy, to be everything and everywhere
in sympathy, and yet content to remain where and what
you are—is not this to know both wisdom and virtue,
and to dwell with happiness? After all, it is not they who
carry flags, but they who look upon it from a private
chamber, who have the fun of the procession. And once
you are at that, you are in the very humour of all social
heresy. It is no time for shuffling, or for big empty words.
If you ask yourself what you mean by fame, riches, or
learning, the answer is far to seek; and you go back into
that kingdom of light imaginations, which seem so vain
in the eyes of Philistines perspiring after wealth, and so
momentous to those who are stricken with the dispro-
portions of the world, and, in the face of the gigantic
stars, cannot stop to split differences between two degrees
of the infinitesimally small, such as a tobacco pipe or the
Roman Empire, a million of money or a fiddlestick's end.

You lean from the window, your last pipe reeking
whitely into the darkness, your body full of delicious
pains, your mind enthroned in the seventh circle of content; when suddenly the mood changes, the weathercock
goes about, and you ask yourself one question more:
whether, for the interval, you have been the wisest philosopher or the most egregious of donkeys. Human experience is not yet able to reply; but at least you have
had a fine moment, and looked down upon all the king-
doms of the earth. And whether it was wise or foolish,
to-morrow's travel will carry you, body and mind, into
some different parish of the infinite.

HILAIRE BELLOC

THE LITTLE RIVER

MEN forget too easily how much the things they see around them in the landscapes of Britain are the work of men. Most of our trees were planted and carefully nurtured by man's hand. Our ploughs for countless centuries have made even the soil of the plains bear human outlines; their groups of hedge and of building, of ridge and of road are very largely the creation of that curious and active breed which was set upon this dull round of the earth to enliven it—which, alone of creatures, speaks and has foreknowledge of death and wonders concerning its origin and its end. It is man that has transformed the surface and the outline of the old countries, and even the rivers carry his handiwork.

There is a little river on my land which very singularly shows the historical truth of what I am here saying. As God made it, it was but a drain rambling through the marshy clay of tangled underwood, sluggishly feeling its way through the hollows in general weathers, scouring in a shapeless flood after the winter rains, dried up and stagnant in isolated pools in our hot summers. Then, no one will ever know how many centuries ago, man came, busy and curious, and doing with his hands. He took my little river; he began to use it, to make it, and to transform it, and to erect of it a human thing. He gave to it its ancient name, which is the ancient name for water, and which you will find scattered upon streams large and small from the Pyrenees up to the Northern Sea and from the west of Germany to the Atlantic. He called it the Adur; therefore pedants pretend that the name is new and not old, for pedants hate the fruitful humour of antiquity.

Well, not only did man give my little river (an inconceivable number of generations ago) the name which it still bears, but he bridged it and he banked it, he scoured it and he dammed it, until he made of it a thing to his own purpose and a companion of the countryside.

With the fortunes of man in our Western and Northern land the fortunes of my little river rose and fell. What the Romans may have done with it we do not know, for a clay soil preserves but little—coins sink in it and the foundations of buildings are lost.

In the breakdown which we call the Dark Ages, and especially perhaps after the worst business of the Danish Invasion, it must have broken back very nearly to the useless and unprofitable thing it had been before man came. The undergrowth, the little oaks and the maples, the coarse grass, the thistle patches, and the briars encroached upon tilled land; the banks washed down, floods carried away the rotting dams, the waterwheels were forgotten and perished. There seem to have been no mills. There is no good drinking water in that land, save here and there at a rare spring, unless you dig a well, and the people of the Dark Ages in Britain, broken by the invasion, dug no wells in the desolation of my valley.

Then came the Norman: the short man with the broad shoulders and the driving energy, and that regal sense of order which left its stamp wherever he marched, from the Grampians to the Euphrates. He tamed that land again, he ploughed the clay, he cut the undergrowth, and he built a great house of monks and a fine church of stone where for so long there had been nothing but flying robbers, outlaws, and the wolves of the weald.

To my little river the Norman was particularly kind. He dug it out and deepened it, he bridged it again, and he sluiced it; it brimmed to its banks, it was once more the companion of men, and, what is more, he dug it out so thoroughly all the twenty miles to the sea that he could even use it for barges and for light boats, so that this head of the stream came to be called Shipley, for goods of ships could be floated, when all this was done, right up to the wharf which the Knights Templar had built above the church to meet the waters of the stream.

All the Middle Ages that fruitfulness and that use

continued. But with the troubles in which the Middle Ages closed and in which so much of our civilization was lost, the little river was once more half abandoned. The church still stood, but stone by stone the great building of the Templars disappeared. The river was no longer scoured; its course was checked by dense bush and reed, the wild beasts came back, the lands of the King were lost. One use remained to the water—the Norman's old canalization was forgotten and the wharf had slipped into a bank of clay, and was now no more than a tumbled field with no deep water standing by. This use was the use of the Hammer Ponds. Here and there the stream was banked up, and the little fall thus afforded was used to work the heavy hammers of the smithies in which the iron of the countryside was worked. For in this clay of ours there was ironstone everywhere, and the many oaks of the weald furnished the charcoal for its smelting. The metal work of the great ships that fought the French, many of their guns also, and bells and railings for London, were smithied or cast at the issue of these Hammer Ponds. But coal came and the new smelting; our iron was no longer worked, and the last usefulness of the little river seemed lost.

Then for two generations all that land lay apart, the stream quite choked or furiously flooding, the paths unworkable in winter: no roads, but only green lanes, and London, forty miles away, unknown.

The last resurrection of the little river has begun to-day. The railway was the first bringer of good news (if you will allow me to be such an apologist for civilization); then came good hard roads in numbers, and quite lately the bicycle, and, last of all, the car. The energy of men reached Adur once again, and once again began the scouring and making of the banks and the harnessing of the water for man; so that, though we have not tackled the canal as we should (that will come), yet with every year the Adur grows more and more of a companion again. It has furnished two fine great lakes for two of my neighbours, and in one place after another they have bridged it as they should, and though clay is a doubtful thing to deal with they have banked it as well.

The other day as I began a new and great and good dam with sluices and with puddled clay behind oak boards and with huge oak uprights and oaken spurs to stand the rush of the winter floods, I thought to myself, working in that shimmering and heated air, how what I was doing was one more of the innumerable things that men had done through time incalculable to make the river their own, and the thought gave me great pleasure, for one becomes larger by mixing with any company of men, whether of our brothers now living or of our fathers who are dead.

This little river—the river Adur before I have done with it—will be as charming and well-bred a thing as the Norman or the Roman knew. It shall bring up properly to well-cut banks. These shall be boarded. It shall have clear depths of water in spite of the clay, and reeds and water-lilies shall grow only where I choose. In every way it shall be what the things of this world were made to be—the servant and the instrument of Man.

H

G. K. CHESTERTON

ON LYING IN BED

LYING in bed would be an altogether perfect and supreme experience if only one had a coloured pencil long enough to draw on the ceiling. This, however, is not generally a part of the domestic apparatus on the premises. I think myself that the thing might be managed with several pails of Aspinall and a broom. Only if one worked in a really sweeping and masterly way, and laid on the colour in great washes, it might drip down again on one's face in floods of rich and mingled colour like some strange fairy rain; and that would have its disadvantages. I am afraid it would be necessary to stick to black and white in this form of artistic composition. To that purpose, indeed, the white ceiling would be of the greatest possible use; in fact it is the only use I think of a white ceiling being put to.

But for the beautiful experiment of lying in bed I might never have discovered it. For years I have been looking for some blank spaces in a modern house to draw on. Paper is much too small for any really allegorical design; as Cyrano de Bergerac says: 'Il me faut des géants.' But when I tried to find these fine clear spaces in the modern rooms such as we all live in I was continually disappointed. I found an endless pattern and complication of small objects hung like a curtain of fine links between me and my desire. I examined the walls; I found them to my surprise to be already covered with wall-paper, and I found the wall-paper to be already covered with very uninteresting images, all bearing a ridiculous resemblance to each other. I could not understand why one arbitrary symbol (a symbol apparently entirely devoid of any religious or philosophical significance) should thus be sprinkled all over my nice walls like a sort of small-pox. The Bible must be referring to wall-papers, I think, when it says 'Use not vain repetitions, as the Gentiles do'. I found the Turkey carpet a mass of unmeaning colours, rather like the Turkish Empire, or like the sweetmeat called Turkish Delight. I do not exactly know what Turkish Delight really is; but I suppose it is Macedonian Massacres. Everywhere that I went forlornly with my pencil or my paint brush, I found that others had unaccountably been before me, spoiling the walls, the curtains, and the furniture with their childish and barbaric designs.

.   .   .   .

Nowhere did I find a really clear space for sketching until this occasion when I prolonged beyond the proper limit the process of lying on my back in bed. Then the light of that white heaven broke upon my vision, that breadth of mere white which is indeed almost the definition of Paradise, since it means purity and also means freedom. But alas! like all heavens, now that it is seen it is found to be unattainable; it looks more austere and more distant than the blue sky outside the window. For my proposal to paint on it with the bristly end of a broom has been discouraged—never mind by whom; by a person debarred from all political rights—and even my minor proposal to put the other end of the broom into the kitchen fire and turn it into charcoal has not been conceded. Yet I am certain that it was from persons in my position that all the original inspiration came for covering the ceilings of palaces and cathedrals with a riot of fallen angels or victorious gods. I am sure that it was only because Michaelangelo was engaged in the ancient and honourable occupation of lying in bed that he ever realized how the roof of the Sistine Chapel might be made into an awful imitation of a divine drama that could only be acted in the heavens.

The tone now commonly taken towards the practice of lying in bed is hypocritical and unhealthy. Of all the marks of modernity that seem to mean a kind of decadence, there is none more menacing and dangerous than the exaltation of very small and secondary matters of conduct at the expense of very great and primary ones, at the expense of eternal ties and tragic human morality. If there is one thing worse than the modern weakening of major morals it is the modern strengthening of minor morals. Thus it is considered more withering to accuse a man of bad taste than of bad ethics. Cleanliness is not next to godliness nowadays, for cleanliness is made an essential and godliness is regarded as an offence. A playwright can attack the institution of marriage so long as he does not misrepresent the manners of society, and I have met Ibsenite pessimists who thought it wrong to take beer but right to take prussic acid. Especially this is so in matters of hygiene; notably such matters as lying in bed. Instead of being regarded, as it ought to be, as a matter of personal convenience and adjustment, it has come to be regarded by many as if it were a part of essential morals to get up early in the morning. It is upon the whole part of practical wisdom; but there is nothing good about it or bad about its opposite.

Misers get up early in the morning; and burglars, I am informed, get up the night before. It is the great peril of our society that all its mechanism may grow more fixed while its spirit grows more fickle. A man's minor actions and arrangements ought to be free, flexible, creative; the things that should be unchangeable are his principles, his ideals. But with us the reverse is true; our views change constantly; but our lunch does not change. Now, I should like men to have strong and rooted conceptions, but as for their lunch, let them have it sometimes in the garden, sometimes in bed, sometimes on the roof, sometimes in the top of a tree. Let them argue from the same first principles, but let them do it in a bed, or a boat, or a balloon. This alarming growth of good habits really means a too great emphasis on those virtues which mere custom can ensure; it means too little emphasis on those virtues which custom can never quite ensure, sudden and splendid virtues of inspired pity or of inspired candour. If ever that abrupt appeal is made to us we may fail. A man can get used to getting up at five o'clock in the morning. A man cannot very well get used to being burnt for his opinions; the first experiment is commonly fatal. Let us pay a little more attention to these possibilities of the heroic and the unexpected. I dare say that when I get out of this bed I shall do some deed of an almost terrible virtue.

For those who study the great art of lying in bed there is one emphatic caution to be added. Even for those who can do their work in bed (like journalists), still more for those whose work cannot be done in bed (as, for example, the professional harpooners of whales), it is obvious that the indulgence must be very occasional. But that is not the caution I mean. The caution is this: if you do lie in bed, be sure you do it without any reason or justification at all. I do not speak, of course, of the seriously sick. But if a healthy man lies in bed, let him do it without a rag of excuse; then he will get up a healthy man. If he does it for some secondary hygienic reason, if he has some scientific explanation, he may get up a hypochondriac.

ROBERT LYND

ON GOOD RESOLUTIONS

THERE is too little respect paid to the good resolutions which are so popular a feature of the New Year. We laugh at the man who is always turning over a new leaf as though he were the last word in absurdity, and we even invent proverbs to discourage him, such as that 'the road to Hell is paved with good intentions'. This makes life extremely difficult for the well-meaning. It robs many of us of the very last of our little store of virtue. Our virtue we have hitherto put almost entirely into our resolutions. To ask us to put it into our actions instead is like asking a man who has for years devoted his genius to literature to switch it off on to marine biology. Nature, unfortunately, has not made us sufficiently accommodating for these rapid changes. She has appointed to each of us his own small plot; has made one of us a poet, another an economist, another a politician—one of us good at making plans, another good at putting them into execution. One feels justified, then, in claiming for the maker of good resolutions a place in the sun. Good resolutions are too delightful a form of morality to be allowed to disappear from a world in which so much of morality is dismal. They are morality at its dawn—morality fresh and untarnished and full of song. They are golden anticipations of the day's work—anticipations of which, alas! the day's work too often proves unworthy. Work, says Amiel somewhere, is vulgarized thought. Work, I prefer to say, is vulgarized good resolutions. There are, no doubt, some people whose resolutions are so natively mediocre that it is no trouble in the world to put them into practice. Promise and perform-ance are in such cases as like as a pair of twins; both are contemptible. But as for those of us whose promises are apt to be Himalayan, how can we expect the little pack-mule of performance to climb to such pathless and giddy heights? Are not the Himalayas in themselves a sufficiently inspiring spectacle—all the more inspiring, indeed, if some peak still remains unscaled, mysterious?

But resolutions of this magnitude belong rather to the region of day-dreams. They take one back to one's childhood, when one longed to win the football cup for one's school team, and, if possible, to have one's leg broken just as one scored the decisive try. Considering that one did not play football, this may surely be regarded as a noble example of an impossible ideal. It has the inaccessibility of a star rather than of a mountain-peak. As one grows older, one's resolutions become earthier. They are concerned with such things as giving up tobacco, taking exercise, answering letters, chewing one's food properly, going to bed before midnight, getting up before noon. This may seem a mean list enough, but there is wonderful comfort to be got out of even a modest good resolution so long as it refers, not to the next five minutes, but to to-morrow, or next week, or next month, or next year, or the year after. How vivid, how beautiful, to-morrow seems with our lordly regiment of good resolutions ready to descend upon it as upon a city seen afar off for the first time! Every day lies before us as wonderful as London lay before Blücher on the night when he exclaimed: 'My God, what a city to loot!' Our life is gorgeous with to-morrows. It is all to-morrows. Good resolutions might be described, in the words in which a Cabinet Minister once described journalism, as the intelligent anticipation of events. They are, however, the intelligent anticipation of events which do not take place. They are the April of virtue with no September following.

On the other hand, there is much to be said for putting a good resolution into effect now and then. There is a brief introductory period in most human conduct, before the novelty has worn off, when doing things is almost, if not quite, as pleasant as thinking about them. Thus, if you make a resolve to get up at seven o'clock every day during the year you should do it on at least one morning. If you do, you will feel so surprised with the world, and so content with your own part in it, that you will decide to get up at seven every morning for the rest of your life. But do not be rash. Getting up early, if you do it seldom enough, is an intoxicating experience. But before long the intoxication fades, and only the habit is left. It was not the elder brother with his habits, but the prodigal with his occasional recurrence into virtue, for whom the fatted calf was killed. Even for the prodigal, when once he had settled down to orderly habits, the supply of fatted calves from his father's farm was bound before long to come to an end.

There are, however, other good resolutions in which it is not so easy to experiment for a single morning. If you resolved to learn German, for instance, there would be very little intoxication to be got out of a single sitting face to face with a German grammar. Similarly, the inventors of systems of exercise for keeping the townsman in condition all remind us that, in order to attain health, we must go on toiling morning after morning at their wretched punchings and twistings and kickings till the end of time. This is an unfair advantage to take of the ordinary maker of good resolutions. He is enticed into the adventure of trying a new thing only to discover that he cannot be said to have tried it until he has tried it on a thousand occasions. Most of us, it may be said at once, are not to be enticed into such matters higher than our knees. We may go so far as to buy the latest book on health or the latest mechanical apparatus to hang on the wall. But soon they become little more than decorations for our rooms. The pair of immense dumb-bells that we got in our boyhood, when we believed that the heavier the dumb-bell the more magnificently would our biceps swell—who would think of taking them from their dusty corner now? Then there was that pair of wooden dumb-bells light as wind, which we tried for awhile on hearing that heavy dumb-bells were a snare and only hardened the muscles without strengthening them. They lie now where the woodlouse may eat them if it has so lowly an appetite. But our good resolutions did really array themselves in colours when the first of the exercisers was invented. There was a thrill in those first mornings when we rose a little earlier than usual and expected to find an inch added to our chest measurement before breakfast. That is always the characteristic of good resolutions. They are founded on a belief in the possibility of performing miracles. If we could swell visibly as a result of a single half-hour's tug at weights and wires, we would all desert our morning's sleep for our exerciser with a will. But the faith that believes in miracles is an easy sort of faith. The faith that goes on believing in the final excellence, though one day shows no obvious advance on another, is the more enviable genius. It is perhaps the rarest thing in the world, and all the good resolutions ever made, if placed end to end, would not make so much as an inch of it. One man I knew who had faith of this kind. He used to practise strengthening his will every evening by buying almonds and raisins or some sort of sweet thing, and sitting down before them by the hour without touching them. And frequently, so he told me, he would repeat over to himself a passage which Poe quotes at the top of one of his stories—'The Fall of the House of Usher', was it not?—beginning 'Great are the mysteries of the will'. I envied him his philosophic grimness: I should never have been able to resist the almonds and raisins. But that incantation from Poe—was not that, too, but a desperate clutching after the miraculous?

There is nothing which men desire more fervently than this mighty will. It may be the most selfish or unselfish of desires. We may long for it for its own sake or for the sake of some purpose which means more to us than praise. We are eager to escape from that continuous humiliation of the promises we have made to ourselves and broken. It is all very well to talk about being baffled to fight better, but that implies a will on the heroic scale. Most of us, as we see our resolutions fly out into the sun, only to fall with broken wings before they have more than begun their journey, are inclined at times to relapse into despair. On the other hand, Nature is prodigal, and in nothing so much as good resolutions. In spite of the experience of half a lifetime of failure, we can still draw upon her for these with the excitement of faith in our hearts. Perhaps there is some instinct for perfection in us which thus makes us deny our past and stride off into the future forgetful of our chains. It is the first step that counts, says the proverb. Alas! we know that that is the step that nearly everybody can take. It is when we are about to take the steps that follow that our ankle feels the drag of old habit. For even those of us who are richest in good resolutions are the creatures of habit just as the baldly virtuous are. The only difference is that we are the slaves of old habits while they are the masters of new ones. . . . On the whole, then, we cannot do better as the New Year approaches than resolve to go out once more in quest of the white flower which has already been allowed to fade too long, where Tennyson placed it, in the late Prince Consort's buttonhole.

EDWARD THOMAS

RAIN

THE prejudice of poets against water has perhaps kept rain out of fashion in literature. It is true that rain is among the subtle, anonymous dramatis personae of *Lear*, and that Milton wove into the harmonies of melancholy 'the minute-drops from off the eaves'. Swift's famous 'Shower' knocks somewhat grossly at the door. 'There never was such a shower since Danae's' ran contemporary compliment. There is, too, an allusion to rain in *Childe Harold*, as a *pianissimo* accompaniment to storms. But it is characteristic of modern poetry, as a criticism of life by livers, that it has left the praise of rain to hop farmers and of mud to shoe-blacks. If literature were faithful to life, there would have been a chorus of benedictions after the rain that whispered on the hansom window-panes and sent the grumbling Thames to sleep with soft hands, as we drove from the play on a Midsummer night; the French Academy would have elected at least one member for his rendering of the meaning of sleet, during a grey and purple sunset over the coast of Brittany. Even at the fireside I am washed by rain until I seem to glimmer and rejoice like the white headstones on the hill!

It is falling now as I sit with paper-spoiling intention, and the sound brings back the rain that used to come from heaven on summer mornings at Oxford, while invisible cattle were lowing and doves cooing, and a distant bell was tolled: brings back the rain in a city street by night, that softened the sky to a deep blue that was the very hue of mercy thrown over the awful darkness; and —gaily, daintily—the drops that came and went (like stars in a restless sky) on the fir-tree foliage as we came to the trout river, in sudden sunlight. Now it is near sunset. The blackbirds are singing lazily in the gardens. The traffic has ceased as if the silence had cried: 'No thoroughfare.' A Circean lady is playing Grieg. She

could turn us into swine; that her quiet smile proclaims:
she does for the time change into gods some of those who
are sitting in the great blue apartment, half shadowed, as
the expression fluctuates, tender, minatory, tumultuous,
hypnotic, vast. Still the rain is falling, and the horse-
chestnuts in the street expand, their leaves shine. Their
size and beauty are as things newly acquired. Two
especially that rise between distant groups of houses fill
the whole space of sky—touch the stars; in a few minutes,
the constellations hang in their branches and swing as the
trees are shaken. The rain has gone to their very hearts.
They sigh tremulously as if the drops moved them with
a tranquil joy. I could wish I were a horse-chestnut
now. . . . In winter I have seen them made much of by
the heavens, and, against the rainy blue, so vast as to
touch the roof of the temple, like the Zeus of Pheidias,
particularly when all day the shower has descended pen-
sively and without wind. Then songs were hushed; the
pools rocked only with smooth leaden waves. Before
evening the rain had worked its spell. Thrushes' songs
filled the hawthorns among the gorse. The wan grass was
beautiful; but for a time the young blades were dominant,
deep green with the depth of night, yet fresh with the
freshness of day; black, dripping trees overhung the
grass, and both had a colour like that of hues and forms
seen through water. All things smiled faintly so that I
seemed to touch the pericardium of eternity. The slight
melancholy and the great solemnity of the rain that had
passed away entered the song of the robin.

Few pictures deal nobly with rain and mud. Yet in
a great city what elvish effects they prepare! Coruscat-
ing, sadly but brilliantly, the mud gravely relieves the
white faces and gaudy raiment that pass by night, and
adds to the dreaminess of a scene, in which the pageant
of life is like a strange flora to the eye. Of all the mud
I have known, the most beautiful is that which is often
to be seen on the bank of Thames below Waterloo Bridge,
lying like a crude monster, while the sunset is rosy and
green and purple on its flanks, and two swans float and

barges heave at rest; or while at dawn the city is all its
own, a quiet grey city that has vanished when the mud
has sunk below the tide.

One shower I remember that wrought magic in a
London garden. A kind of judicious neglect by the owner
had made the garden a kindly party to any unusual trick
of the elements. On the lawn was a sundial that made
Time an alluring toy. At the bottom of the garden, beyond the lawn, was an enclosed space of warm rank
grasses, and rising over them a vapour of cow-parsley
flowers. A white steam from the soil faintly misted the
grass to the level of the tallest buttercups. Rain was
falling, and the grasses and overhanging elm trees seemed
to be suffering for their quietness and loneliness, to be
longing for something, as perhaps Eden also dropped
'some natural tears' when left a void. A hot, not quite
soothing, perfume crept over the lawn. All night I was
haunted by those elms which appeared as grey women
in cloaks of that strange mist. For the time that garden
was the loneliest place on earth, and I loved and feared
its loneliness.

Of rain seen from indoors, falling on a broad rich land
of grass and trees, or seen (from heavenly altitudes) falling
on the grey and blue slates of a town I dare not speak.
But I have known the rain, hissing on the lawn, complete
the luxury of tea at Oxford in November, when the heart
is fresh from walking. There is a generous fire; seven-
league slippers on the feet; ' .u buttered brown toast;
and, as evening changes from grey to grey in quiet
crescendo, still the rain.

In this London garden there was one day which I may
not omit, for the rain that buried it said many things
which I have copied.

The shadow of the lime trees lay soft upon the grass,
wonderfully soft because of the shy early sunlight. A bird
sang such blithe notes as wakened the soul, disrobing it
of the dishonours and disgusts of ages, restoring it to
Paradise. From a corner of the garden I could see, over
many steeples and chimneys, the side of a great wave of

land, fledged with a few white cloudlets; and as yet I could not say whether these were of snow or blackthorn flowers. Fainter still, among distant trees, I saw a doubtful glimmer which might be the forward sweeping hem of vernal splendour. In such moments of doubt I have found the calendar's positive announcement of Spring a solace. A mist muffled the angles of the landscape, a mist where the whole force of Spring might lie in ambush. The sun had burnt for an hour like the fire of a thrifty candle. Presently it flushed (it almost crackled like a faggot) with a good-humoured lustihead. Then I knew that in the grass the dewy charities of the south winds were beginning to tell, and that the haze had fostered that slumbrous warmth in which chaffinches love to sing. Through the grey air at first the sky was invisible, save a misted blue pane here and there appearing, and vanishing, and engrailed by the grey cloud. Some windows northward glowed. Something undefinable that was Spring's and Dawn's richly mounted everything; it entered the new stone church and gave it centuries backward and forward of glory and repose. Even the shadows on a dusty road were mysterious as shadow on deep water, and had an azure unknown before. And still the blackbirds sang:

> High trolollie lollie loe
> High trolollie lee.
> Tho' others think they have as much
> Yet he that says so lies.
> Then come away,
> Turn country man with me.

A wind just lifted the coltsfoot down. Such a wind it was as brings to corners where the willow-wrens never wander a sound like the song of willow-wrens and all that their bland southern voices mean among English trees. It comes in March from between the South and the East, and passes into the cold and odourless meadows, with the odour of all the flowers of the orient and the sweetness of the sea.

My path lay between rows of houses that were hidden by almond flowers among black boughs. If I paused—

and the wind dropped—I could just detect the reluctant
savour of struggling green life. Then the 'lane' became
the bordering road of a common. Here the sun was the
genius of a company of haggard poplars in whose branches
it seemed to hang, and the paths are haunted by ghosts
of divers faces—O Memory!

> Tuis hic omnia plena
> Muneribus.

One of these ghosts—the rain was beginning to hiss in
the trees and patter on the dead leaves below—was of an
old man who had played Edmund in his youth. Beaten
by a slow mortal disease in his prime, he had lived happily
in the midst of friends who never abated the services
which his gracious feebleness exacted and made appear
a duty. He who should have died first survived them all.
His mind nodded and slept, leaving a childishness that
was not happy. All the pleasant valetudinarian space
disappeared from his memory; the tumultuous early days
returned, and at intervals he strayed amidst the pageant
in which the figures of Lear and Richard the Second
towered with minatory pomp. For his part had ever been
traitorous and base. The evil acted 'in his days of nature'
haunted him fearfully. In a great voice (so that he used
to say: 'I fear my mother hears me') he would repeat
the speech of Lear: 'Howl, howl, howl, howl, Oh! ye are
men of stones,' as often he had heard it when, as Edmund,
he was borne off before the end: he seemed to whimper
behind the stage, crying bitterly to be admitted to die
before the King. Luckily, before his death all became
dark. It was with surprise that I heard he was dead.
For years he seemed not to have lived. . . .

Now the road went near several great houses, of a kind
which rain makes eloquent. And the rain was falling then
with a sound like the silence of a multitude. They were
not the old, beautiful houses of London, but such as were
built not more than sixty years ago for some one grown
suddenly rich. The old houses can always chatter of what
has fallen from them by indiscreet neglect or foolish care,

and all must regret the blotting of the little unnecessary trifles that were part of their nobility, like the grassy spaces between the garden wall and the public road, where the fowls paraded, and the ivy was plaited with periwinkle to the edge of the macadam. These middle-aged houses make no such appeal. They gibber in premature senility, between tragedy and comedy. Nobody will live there now; the gardens are feeble and disordered, and the dahlias fade one by one. Passers-by laugh at their 'style'. Even the creepers have taken no hold of the wall and have fallen dishevelled. I do not believe the former occupants ever come a little way out of their path to see their house. Yonder were the gaudy doors, and blinds still hanging; the romantic name on the folding gates; and I remembered the autumn rain in which they took heart. Each was the gloomier for the one lamp glimmering near the gate; the soiled crimson leaves were shaken out over the path; the starlings screamed mechanically; the bleared sunset was swallowed up in rain. And in that hour the house, once an anachronism, a mixture of parts of several incongruous styles, seemed to have grown very old, and against the wildly moving sky and stars it gained an indubitable style, that of Stonehenge and the mountain crag—the natural style, the immortal style of things too old.

Beyond these houses lay the Little House, and behind a high exclusive fence, a holly hedge and a lawn. It was empty. Its orchards were praised almost as they deserved, its rent lowered, in advertisements; nobody came. Yet the lawn was always green; a gardener—or who?—kept sharp the angles which it made with the drive. The crocuses came out and lasted till the west wind spilt their petals in the deep grass. The only sign of neglect was the temerity of the ivy, which crept through the chinks of the door, through the keyhole, into the letter-box.

The rooms could be dimly seen from without, especially the great shaded children's nursery that faced the north and has said to me as I have passed:

I know the secret of the unhappiness of childhood. A

fate abides with me and through her I know the laws that mingle with the roses of life the lilies of death. I have made festal days awful. Many a sad dreamer curses the shadows that he used to see falling on my walls in early firelight.

And it continued until I wished for a Blakesmoor where I could quiet my alarms. As a rule there was no hint of mysterious inhabitants. The emptiness was far more mysterious. It was wonderful to see how wild the garden looked after a short desertion—not disordered or weedy, but wild—though the flowers were of the daintiest and most elaborate kinds. Years ago I heard some one playing 'Didone Abandonnata' in the Little House, and in the garden the echoes struck something that repeats them still.

To us, as children, it used to be a famous day when a new tenant came to this house. We had a cruel standard of fitness to apply to whosoever came. Best of all we liked the ancient who lived in one room of it, kept no servants, put up no curtains, and in fact left the house exactly as we wished. We used to hear him singing in a cheerful rasping voice under the big cedar when he thought no one was near. When he quitted it, sitting among his furniture in an open cart, we implored him to stay. For a time we were alternately sorry and pleased at the emptiness of the house. We used to save our pocket-money continuously for whole months, to buy the freehold. And so we came to have a sense of possession, if not of occupation, which (we thought) was stronger because it was not known. To the sequestered Sylvans whose escaping footsteps were heard in very early morning we prayed

> Be present aye with favourable feet,
> And, all profane, audience far remove.

So intimate we grew that the garden seemed to understand us. I would that I could understand it in return.

On Spring days—like this—when a grass scent came into the streets as if the fields and woods were insurgent, near at hand, it was to the garden we went, counted

daffodils and lime leaves, listening for the new-come
martins that sang before they were seen, in the dark. In
these early visits we found more in the garden than was
in the articles of sale. So we hated the rhododendrons
that were planted by a later tenant. He took an interest
in the garden that was horrible; frivolous music was
played in the house. Nevertheless, in spite of the
laughter, the splendour, and the glossy carriage, the
house had a defiant air, hating the young gods and god-
desses that supplanted the Olympians it once knew. All
its peers in the neighbourhood had given way to villas;
I thought that perchance it was time for the Little House
to go. At evening the thought grew stronger; the house
itself cried

> Now mark me how I will undo myself.

It went on

> God pardon all oaths that are broke to me

as if perhaps it knew that I had been vain enough to
think I could have lived there happily, as if it cared for
the foolish ritual of my sorrow. If it were destroyed, no
one could assail my ownership. I might be content. *Car
il en est toujours qu'on peut aimer.* . . . Yet I am not sure
that I would have possessed it actually. One day two of
us were looking over the gate gathering honey with our
eyes, when a gracious little girl came smiling towards us;
we slunk away. A little later she surprised us on tiptoe
at the same place and at her invitation we entered the
garden for the first time. We were persuaded to sit down
near the lilacs. But we did not look round; left alone
for a moment, we planned an escape. Even when she
came out with a tray and sat beside us, we were not
happy. I remember that we whispered together, and the
child laughed and tried to put us at our ease. My friend
said with a voice of discovery: 'They have tea here.' We
were near disillusion; only, we did not know!

I have said there was a common next to the house.
The garden was more ours than that. Independence
commonly means a state in which we never know on

whom we depend; the term 'common' was false, and those
who walked on it knew no such liberty as we. The garden
belonged to us as truly as the world to the children who,
in a great library, colour the globe, red, green, and blue,
for Mary, Arthur, and Dick. On the common there were
'strange fetters to the feet, strange manacles to the
hands'. If any should wonder at this let them go to the
garden at evening. A half-moon is alone in the sky. Is
it green or is it white? Here and there clusters of poplars
vein the horizon. At that hour the waving trees are as
delicate as grasses. Some windows are lit. Here a song
is ending; there a door is violently shut; but already
London is growing silent. The sounds are so faint that
if I pause to listen and unravel them, I can hear my
heart, the ticking of my watch, but not the enormous
city. Go to the garden and see, in the shadow of a cedar,
the apple-blossom glow.

MAX BEERBOHM

ON GOING BACK TO SCHOOL

THE other evening, at about seven o'clock, I was in a swift hansom. My hat was tilted at a gay angle, and, for all I was muffled closely, my gloves betokened a ceremonious attire. I was smoking *la cigarette d'appétit*, and was quite happy. Outside Victoria my cab was stopped by a file of other cabs, that were following one another in at the main entrance of the station. I noticed, on one of them, a small hat-box, a newish trunk, and a corded play-box, and I caught one glimpse of a very small, pale boy in a billicock-hat. He was looking at me through the side-window. If Envy was ever inscribed on any face, it was inscribed on the face of that very small, pale boy. 'There,' I murmured, 'but for the grace of God, goes Max Beerbohm!'

My first thought, then, was for myself. I could not but plume me on the contrast of my own state with his. But, gradually, I became fulfilled with a very great compassion for him. I understood the boy's Envy so well. It was always the most bitter thing, in my own drive to the station, to see other people, quite happy, as it seemed, with no upheaval of their lives; people in cabs, who were going out to dinner and would sleep in London; grown-up people! Than the impotent despair of those drives—I had exactly fifteen of them—I hope that I shall never experience a more awful emotion. Those drives have something, surely, akin with drowning. In their course the whole of a boy's home-life passes before his eyes, every phase of it standing out against the black curtain of his future. The author of *Vice-Versa* has well analysed the feeling, and he is right, I think, in saying that all boys, of whatsoever temperament, are preys to it. Well do I remember how, on the last day of the holidays, I used always to rise early, and think that I had got twelve more whole hours of happiness, and how those hours used to

pass me with mercifully slow feet. . . . Three more hours!
. . . Sixty more minutes! . . . Five! . . . I used to draw upon
my tips for a first-class ticket, that I might not be plunged
suddenly among my companions, with their hectic and
hollow mirth, their dreary disinterment of last term's
jokes. I used to revel in the thought that there were
many stations before G——. . . . The dreary walk, with my
small bag, up the hill! I was not one of those who made
a rush for the few cabs. . . . The awful geniality of the
House Master! The jugs in the dormitory! . . . Next
morning, the bell that woke me! The awakening!

Not that I had any special reason for hating school!
Strange as it may seem to my readers, I was not unpopular
there. I was a modest, good-humoured boy. It is Oxford
that has made me insufferable. At school, my character
remained in a state of undevelopment. I had a few
misgivings, perhaps. In some respects, I was always too
young, in others, too old, for a perfect relish of the
convention. As I hovered, in grey knickerbockers, on a
cold and muddy field, round the outskirts of a crowd that
was tearing itself limb from limb for the sake of a leathern
bladder, I would often wish for a nice, warm room and
a good game of hunt-the-slipper. And, when we sallied
forth, after dark, in the frost, to the swimming-bath, my
heart would steal back to the fireside in Writing School
and the plot of Miss Braddon's latest novel. Often, since,
have I wondered whether a Spartan system be really
well for youths who are bound mostly for Capuan
Universities. It is true, certainly, that this system makes
Oxford or Cambridge doubly delectable. Undergraduates
owe their happiness chiefly to the consciousness that they
are no longer at school. The nonsense which was knocked
out of them at school is all put gently back at Oxford or
Cambridge. And the discipline to which they are subject
is so slight that it does but serve to accentuate their real
freedom. The sudden reaction is rather dangerous, I
think, to many of them.

Even now, much of my complacency comes of having
left school. Such an apparition as that boy in the hansom

makes me realize my state more absolutely. Why, after all, should I lavish my pity on him and his sorrows? *Dabit deus his quoque finem.* I am at a happier point in Nature's cycle. That is all. I have suffered every one of his ordeals, and I do not hesitate to assure him, if he chance to see this essay of mine, how glad I am that I do not happen to be his contemporary. I have no construe of Xenophon to prepare for to-morrow morning, nor any ode of Horace to learn, painfully, by heart. I assure him that I have no wish nor any need to master, as he has, at this moment, the intricate absurdities of that proposition in the second book of Euclid. I have no locker, with my surname printed on it and a complement of tattered school-books. I burnt all my school-books when I went up to Oxford. Were I to meet, now, any one of those masters who are monsters to you, my boy, he would treat me even more urbanely, it may be, than I should treat him. When he sets you a hundred lines, you write them without pleasure, and he tears them up. When I, with considerable enjoyment and at my own leisure, write a hundred lines or so, they are printed for all the world to admire, and I am paid for them enough to keep you in pocket-money for many terms. I write at a comfortable table, by a warm fire, and occupy an arm-chair, whilst you are sitting on a narrow form. My boots are not made 'for school-wear', nor do they ever, like yours, get lost in a litter of other boots in a cold boot-room. In a word, I enjoy myself immensely. To-night, I am going to a theatre. Afterwards, I shall sup somewhere and drink wine. When I come home and go to bed, I shall read myself to sleep with some amusing book. . . . You will have torn yourself from your bed, at the sound of a harsh bell, have washed, quickly, in very cold water, have scurried off to Chapel, gone to first school and been sent down several places in your form, tried to master your next construe, in the interval of snatching a tepid break-fast, been kicked by a bigger boy, and had a mint of horrible experiences, long before I, your elder by a few years, have awakened, very gradually, to the tap of knuckles on the panel of my bedroom-door. I shall make a leisurely toilet. I shall descend to a warm breakfast, open one of the little budgets which my 'damned good-natured friend', Romeike, is always sending me, and glance at that morning paper which appeals most surely to my sense of humour. And when I have eaten well of all the dishes on the table, I shall light a cigarette. Through the haze of its fragrant smoke, I shall think of the happy day that is before me.

NOTES

FRANCIS BACON

FRANCIS BACON (1561–1626) —called by Pope the 'wisest, brightest, meanest of mankind'—published his *Essays* in the reign of Elizabeth, while he was Queen's Counsel. In the reign of James I he became successively Attorney-General and Lord Chancellor, and was raised to the peerage, first as Lord Verulam and afterwards as Viscount St. Albans. While Lord Chancellor he was charged with bribery. He confessed he was guilty of 'corruption and neglect', and was deprived of his post, fined, and disabled from sitting in parliament. He died five years later.

His best-known literary work, after the *Essays*, is the *New Atlantis*—an account of a 'Utopia'. As a philosopher it was his ambition to create a new system of thought, to replace that of Aristotle, based on a right interpretation of nature. The chief works in which he expressed his philosophical ideas were the *Advancement of Learning* and (in Latin) the *Novum Organum*.

Of Friendship (pp. 9–15)

Page 9, line 1. *that spake it.* Aristotle, *Politics*, I. ii. 14.

l. 10. *conversation.* Manner of living.

l. 11. *Epimenides.* A Greek poet and mystic of the sixth century B.C.

l. 12. *Candian.* Candia was the old name of the island of Crete.

Numa. The second King of Rome and the founder of religious rites.

Empedocles. A Greek philosopher of the fifth century B.C.

l. 13. *Apollonius.* A magician of the first century B.C.

l. 18. *tinkling cymbal.* 1 Cor. xiii. 1.

l. 19. *Magna civitas, &c.* 'A great city is great solitude.'

l. 33. *sarza.* Sarsaparilla.

l. 34. *castoreum.* A drug obtained from the beaver. (Not the same as the modern drug, castor oil, which is of vegetable origin.)

P. 10, l. 13. *sorteth to.* Results in.

l. 15. *privadoes.* A Spanish word.

l. 18. *participes curarum.* 'Partners in their cares.'

l. 30. *pursuit.* Support.

P. 11. *Augustus . . . Tiberius Caesar . . . Septimius Severus . . . Trajan . . . Marcus Aurelius.* Roman Emperors.

l. 14. *Haec pro amicitia, &c.* 'On account of our friendship I have not concealed these things.'

l. 34. *Comineus.* Philippe de Comines (1445–1509), councillor to Charles the Bold of Burgundy, and afterwards to Louis XI.

P. 12, l. 4. *Pythagoras.* A Greek philosopher of the fifth century B.C.

l. 39. *cloth of Arras.* This quotation by Bacon, from a passage in the translation by Sir Thomas North (1535–1601) of the *Life of Themistocles* (514–449 B.C.) by Plutarch (first century A.D.), contains an anachronism, Cloth of Arras being a term originally applied in the Middle Ages to a tapestry made at Arras, in France.

P. 13, l. 7. *whetteth his wits.* He uses his friend, whose wit is dull, for sharpening his wits on.

l. 8. *were better relate himself.* Had better talk.

l. 14. *Heraclitus.* A Greek philosopher of the fifth century B.C.

Dry light. Heraclitus's phrase is 'the dry soul'—which Bacon elsewhere refers to as the light of the pure intellect, unmoistened by the affections.

l. 37. *St. James.* I. 23.

l. 38. *presently.* Immediately.

P. 14, l. 3. *four and twenty letters.* In Bacon's time I and J were not differentiated, nor U and V.

P. 15, l. 14. *a man's person.* The part he plays.

l. 15. *proper.* Peculiar to himself.

l. 17. *upon terms.* Under a truce.

l. 18. *as it sorteth with.* As suits.

JOSEPH ADDISON

JOSEPH ADDISON, essayist, poet, and statesman, was born in 1672. He was educated at Charterhouse and Queen's College, Oxford. In 1705 he was appointed Secretary to the Lord Lieutenant of Ireland. His writings up to this time had included a poem, *The Campaign*, in honour of the battle of Blenheim. In 1709 he contributed to Steele's paper, the *Tatler*, and in 1711 with Steele he produced the *Spectator*, in which appeared his famous 'Coverley Papers'. His play *Cato* was acted with great success. In 1706 he married the Countess of Warwick; retired from office two years later on a handsome pension; and in the following year died.

Sir Roger at Church (pp. 16–18)

P. 16, ll. 1–2. '*Aθανάτους μὲν*, &c. ' In the first place honour the immortal Gods as is appointed by law.' *Pythagoras*: see note to p. 12, l. 4.

P. 18, l. 6. *clerk's place*, The post of lay officer of a parish church.

l. 9. *incumbent*. Occupant of the clerk's place. Now used only of a clergyman.

Meditations in Westminster Abbey (pp. 19–22)

P. 19, ll. 1–5. *Pallida mors*. ' Pale death approaching with impartial tread knocks alike at the cottage of the poor and the palace of the King. O Sestius, you are fortune's favourite; but life's short span forbids us to enter on far-reaching hopes. Soon night will be upon you, and the shadow-world men speak of, and the unsubstantial house of Pluto.' (Horace, *Odes*, I. iv.)

l. 29. '*the path of an arrow.*' Wisdom, v. 12.

P. 20, l. 28. The scene of the victory of Marlborough, 1704.

l. 38. *Sir Cloudesley Shovel*. 1650–1707. He began his career as a cabin-boy.

P. 21, l. 16. *rostral crowns*. Crowns decorated with naval emblems. (*Rostrum*, Lat., the beak of a ship.)

OLIVER GOLDSMITH

OLIVER GOLDSMITH, the son of an Irish clergyman, was born in 1728. He took his degree at Trinity College, Dublin, and studied medicine at Edinburgh University, though he never practised as a physician except in two short snatches. In 1755 he went off wandering on the Continent, and after a year returned to London in destitution. Throughout his life he was extravagant when he earned anything—and when not spending he drudged. He contributed to magazines, and in 1759 he published his *Enquiry into the Present State of Polite Learning*. A few years later his *Chinese Letters* appeared (subsequently reissued as *The Citizen of the World*), and his poem *The Traveller*, which was highly praised by Dr. Johnson, who befriended him. In 1766 his famous novel, *The Vicar of Wakefield*, was published, followed by the production at Covent Garden of his plays, *The Good Natur'd Man* and *She Stoops to Conquer*. In 1770 his poem *The Deserted Village* appeared. Four years later, in 1774, at the age of 46, he died. He had not married. He was buried in the Temple Church. There is a monument to him in Westminster Abbey. Dr. Johnson composed the epitaph, which contains the well-known words 'Nihil quod tetigit non ornavit'—'There was nothing he touched that he did not adorn.'

Beau Tibbs, a Character (pp. 23–5)

P. 24, l. 20. *squeezed a lemon.* When making punch.

To the Printer (pp. 26–8)

This essay is supposed to be a letter written as a contribution to a paper. In Goldsmith's time printing, publishing, and bookselling were not such separate businesses as they are to-day.

P. 26, l. 2. *Common-Council man.* A member of the City Council.

l. 10. *Bristol stones.* A kind of rock-crystal, found near Bristol.

P. 27, l. 22. *mobbed up.* Hooded, muffled.

l. 33. *Bartholomew Fair.* Held from 1133, until 1855, on St. Bartholomew's Day (24th August), in West Smithfield, London.

CHARLES LAMB

CHARLES LAMB was born in 1775. He was educated at Christ's Hospital (then in London), where he met Coleridge. He left school at fourteen, and was employed first in the South Sea House, and then in the East India House, where he remained over twenty years. There was insanity in his family. Lamb himself was a short time in an asylum in 1795. In 1796 his mother was killed by his sister Mary in a fit of madness; Lamb undertook to be his sister's guardian, and lived with her all his life. He did not marry.

In 1796 he contributed to Coleridge's first volume of verse. He wrote for the newspapers; published a blank-verse play; and had a farce produced at Drury Lane, which was a failure. In 1807 his well-known *Tales from Shakespeare*, by himself and his sister, was published; and a year later his *Specimens of English Dramatic Poets contemporary with Shakespeare*. His chief fame rests on the essays which he began contributing to the *London Magazine* in 1820, signed ' Elia '.

In 1825 he retired on an ample pension. He died in 1834, and was buried at Edmonton.

Christ's Hospital Five-and-Thirty Years Ago (pp. 29–42)

P. 29, Title. *Christ's Hospital.* The Blue-coat School was founded by Edward VI in 1552. The boys still wear long blue coats with yellow stockings. In 1902 the school was removed from Newgate Street in London to Horsham in Sussex. A part of the old site is now occupied by the General Post Office.

In this essay Lamb partly ascribes to himself ('Elia') the experiences of Coleridge, who entered the School at the same time as Lamb, though he was nearly three years older.

l. 1. *Mr. Lamb's Works.* This is a red herring drawn by Lamb to conceal his identity. An essay called 'Recollections of Christ's Hospital' was included in the *Works* of Charles Lamb (1818). The present essay appeared first in the *London Magazine* two years later, under his pseudonym of ' Elia '.

l.20. *piggins.* Small wooden vessels bound with hoops.
pitched. Covered with tar.

l. 25. *Temple.* Lamb's father was clerk, and his mother housekeeper, to a Bencher of the Temple, Samuel Salt, M.P., in whose chambers the Lamb family lived.

l. 26. *banyan days.* A nautical term for days on which no meat is served.

l. 28. *double-refined.* Sugar.

l. 31. *caro equina.* Horse flesh.

P. 30, l. 8. *good old relative.* Lamb's aunt, Sarah.

l. 11. *the Tishbite.* Elijah.

l. 33. *Calne in Wiltshire.* A fiction to conceal the identity of Coleridge, who was born at Ottery St. Mary in Devonshire.

P. 31, l. 25. *Lions in the Tower.* There used to be a menagerie in the Tower, which was removed in 1831 to the Zoological Gardens.

l. 28. *presented us to the foundation.* Admission to Christ's Hospital is possible only through nomination by one of the governors. Lamb was nominated by a friend of Samuel Salt (see note to p. 29, l. 25).

P. 32, l. 14. *Nevis . . . St. Kitts.* Islands in the West Indies.

l. 17. *Nero.* Emperor of Rome (A.D. 54–68).

l. 26. *cry roast meat.* Proclaim his good luck.

Caligula's minion. Caligula, Emperor of Rome (A.D. 37–41), had his favourite horse made Consul.

l. 28. *waxing fat, and kicking.* Deut. xxxii. 15.

l. 31. *blew such a ram's horn blast.* Joshua vi. 4.

l. 34. *Smithfield.* The meat market.

P. 33, l. 7. *Verrio.* An Italian painter (1634–1707).

l. 14. *To feed our mind &c.* Virgil, *Aeneid,* i. 464.

ll. 23–4. *'Twas said &c. . . . Antony and Cleopatra,* i, iv. 67–8.

P. 35, l. 29. *'watchet-weeds.'* Blue clothes.

l. 34. *disfigurements in Dante.* Dante in the *Inferno* describes men who are disfigured in punishment for their sins.

l. 38. note *Howard's.* John Howard, the prison-reformer (1726–90), whose statue is in St. Paul's Cathedral.

P. 36, l. 2. *L's.* See note to p. 29, l. 1.

l. 11. *ultima supplicia.* Extreme punishments.

P. 37, l. 10. *'like a dancer.'* Antony and Cleopatra, iii. xi. 35–6.

l. 21. *'insolent Greece or haughty Rome.'* Jonson, 'Lines on Shakespeare'.

l. 22. *Peter Wilkins.* *The Adventures of Peter Wilkins*, by Robert Paltock. (1697–1767). The two other books mentioned are also tales of adventure, of less merit, and now forgotten.

l. 26. *parentheses.* A comparison of the two sides of the string figure in a cat's-cradle, and their sharp bend inward at each end, with the brackets which enclose a parenthesis.

l. 31. *Rousseau and John Locke.* Rousseau (1712–78) and Locke (1632–1704) both advocated educational methods which should give play to children's inclinations.

P. 38, l. 4. *Phaedrus.* A Latin writer of fables in verse, of the first century A.D.

l. 11. *Helots.* Slaves to the Spartans, who used to exhibit a drunken Helot to their sons as a warning.

l. 16. *Xenophon.* The Greek historian—author of the *Anabasis*—of the fourth century B.C.

l. 17. *the Samite.* Pythagoras (see note to p. 12, l. 4), of Samos, who prescribed silence to his students in his presence until they had attended his lectures for five years.

l. 18. *Goshen.* Where the Israelites lived during their bondage in Egypt. It was exempted from the plagues (*Exodus* viii).

l. 22. *Gideon's miracle. Judges* vi. 37, 38.

l. 30. '*playing holiday.*' First *Henry IV*, i. ii. 227.

l. 34. *Ululantes.* Souls wailing in Tartarus, the underworld of classical mythology.

l. 37. *scrannel pipes.* Milton, *Lycidas*, 124.

P. 39, l. 37 note. *Garrick.* David Garrick (1717–79), the famous actor.

l. 2. *Flaccus's.* Horace (Quintus Horatius Flaccus), *Satires*, ii. vii. 35.

tristis severitas &c. 'A gloomy sternness in his face' (from the *Andria* of Terence, 195–150 B.C.).

l. 3. *inspicere in patinas.* 'To look into your saucepans' (from Terence's *Adelphi*).

l. 5. *vis.* Power.

l. 8. *caxon.* Wig.

l. 11. *No comet &c.* Comets were supposed to forebode misfortunes.

l. 25. *rabidus furor.* Mad rage.

l. 28. *Debates.* Parliamentary Debates.

P. 40, l. 12. *literary life. Biographia Literaria*, Ch. i.

l. 14. *Country Spectator.* A weekly periodical edited and mostly written by T. F. Middleton (see p. 41. l. 4).

l. 23. *Grecian.* The top class at Christ's Hospital are called 'Grecians'.

l. 25. *T—e.* This person, and all the others in the rest of the essay mentioned by Lamb under initials, have been identified. See *Essays of Elia,* edited by C. O. Williams (Clarendon Press).

P. 41, l. 9. *regni novitas.* Newness of his kingdom. (Virgil, *Aeneid,* i. 562).

l. 11. *Jewel.* John Jewell (1522–71), Bishop of Salisbury, and author of *Apologia pro Ecclesia Anglicana.*

Hooker. Richard Hooker (1554–1600), author of *The Laws of Ecclesiastical Polity.*

l. 14. *watered.* Nourished, tended. Cf. 1 Corinthians iii. 6.

l. 20. *'Finding some of Edward's race', &c.* Matthew Prior (1664–1721), *Carmen Saeculare for* 1700, stanza 8.

l. 23. *Fiery column.* Exodus xiii. 21–2.

l. 29. *Mirandola.* Pico, Prince of Mirandola in North Italy, famous for his learning (1463–94).

l. 30. *Iamblicus, or Plotinus.* Greek philosophers of the Neoplatonic School in the fourth century A.D.

l. 33. *Pindar.* The Greek lyric poet of the sixth century B.C.

Grey Friars. Christ's Hospital was on the site of an old Grey Friar's monastery dissolved by Henry VIII.

l. 36. *Fuller.* Thomas Fuller (1608–61), divine and historian. The passage which follows is an adaptation from a description in his *Worthies of England.*

P. 42, l. 13. *Nireus formosus.* 'Beautiful Nireus', the King of Naxos, described by Homer as the most beautiful of the Greek heroes before Troy (*Iliad,* ii. 673).

l. 17. *bl—.* Blast.

l. 20. *Elia.* See p. 142, note on 'Christ's Hospital'.

l. 31. *Hertford.* Hertford Grammar School.

The Convalescent (pp. 43–7)

P. 43, l. 5. *this month.* This essay was published first in the *London Magazine,* which appeared monthly.

l. 24. *Mare Clausum.* 'Closed Sea': that part of a sea within which a particular country has sovereign rights.

l. 28. *the Two Tables of the Law.* Exodus xxxi. 18.

l. 35. *refreshing.* Giving a 'refresher'—an extra fee to counsel in a prolonged case.

P. 44, l. 15. *honing.* Grumbling.

P. 46, l. 19. *Lernaean pangs.* An allusion to the pain caused by the arrows which had been dipped by Hercules in the poison of the Lernaean snake. Philoctetes, on his way to the siege of Troy, accidentally trod on one of them, and was incapacitated by the wound for ten years.

l. 39. *What a speck &c.* Quotation unidentified. One editor has conjectured First *Henry IV,* iii. iii. 1; another *Lear,* iv. vi. 17.

P. 47, l. 4. *In articulo mortis.* At the point of death.

l. 13. *hypochondriac flatus.* It has been suggested that Lamb is speaking with medical exactitude of flatulence in the abdomen (the 'hypochondria' are parts of the abdominal region); more probably he means, metaphorically, the 'morbid distension' of the invalid's self-consciousness.

l. 16. *Tityus.* A giant, slain by Zeus, whose body covered nine acres.

WILLIAM HAZLITT

WILLIAM HAZLITT was born in 1778. He was educated for the Unitarian Ministry, but later he studied painting, contributed to magazines, and devoted himself to literature. He had many friends, including Coleridge and Lamb. In some ways he was a volatile and unbalanced person, as is shown by his matrimonial adventures. He married in 1808; in 1822 he divorced his wife; in the following year he was concerned in a love affair (which formed the subject of a book he wrote); in 1823, at the age of 45, he married again, a widow; in 1824 his wife left him.

He died in 1834. On his deathbed he exclaimed to those present—'Well, I've had a happy life', and turning his head to the wall never spoke another word. His writings include *The Characters of Shakespeare's Plays, Lectures on the English Poets, Table Talk, The Spirit of the Age.*

The Indian Jugglers (pp. 48–64)

P. 50, l. 29 note. *Peter Pindar.* The nom-de-plume of John Wolcot (1738–1819), a writer of satires.

l. 30. *Mr. Opie.* John Opie (1761–1807).

P. 51, l. **4.** *Sadler's Wells.* A theatre in Clerkenwell.

P. 52, l. **17.** *Juggernaut.* A Hindu god. At a yearly festival his image is carried on a car through the city. At one time worshippers used to throw themselves under this, in the faith that their souls would thus go to Heaven.

P. 53, l. **3.** *Ivanhoe.* Ch. xiii.

l. **21.** '*human face divine.*' Milton *Paradise Lost*, iii. 44.

l. **25.** *Reynolds.* Sir Joshua Reynolds, the famous portrait-painter (1723–92).

l. **37.** *H——s and H——s.* There are several painters contemporary with Hazlitt whose names begin with ' H '.

P. 54, l. **1.** '*in tones and gestures hit.*' Cf. Milton, *Paradise Regained*, iv. 255.

l. **2.** *To snatch the grace &c.* Pope, *Essay on Criticism*, 153.

l. **6.** '*commercing with the skies.*' Milton, *Il Penseroso*, 38.

ll. **33–4.** *And visions, &c.* From a letter by the poet Gray to Horace Walpole (September 1737), and itself perhaps an adaptation of Virgil, *Aeneid*, vi. 282–4.

P. 55, l. **6.** *Thrills in each nerve.* Cf. Pope, *Essay on Man*, i. 218.

l. **25.** '*half flying, half on foot.*' Milton, *Paradise Lost*, ii. 940.

P. 56, l. **3.** *I know an individual.* Leigh Hunt.

l. **13.** *nugae canorae.* Tuneful trifles. Horace, *Ars Poetica*, 322.

l. **14.** *Rochester.* John Wilmot, Earl of Rochester (1647–80), the profligate courtier and poet.

Surrey. Henry Howard, Earl of Surrey (1517–47), who was executed by Henry VIII. He was the first to use blank verse in five iambic feet in English poetry, and he introduced the Sonnet from Italy into England.

l. **29.** *Themistocles.* The Athenian statesman and general (525–459 B.C.).

P. 57, l. **39.** *Jedediah Buxton.* An ignorant and dense Yorkshireman (1707–72), who nevertheless had prodigious powers of mental calculation.

P. 58, l. **1.** *Napier's bones.* An apparatus for calculating, designed by John Napier (1550–1617), the inventor of logarithms.

l. 6. *Newton.* Sir Isaac Newton (1642–1727), author of the *Principia* and discoverer of gravitation.

l. 11. *Molière.* The French dramatist (1622–73).

l. 12. *author of Don Quixote.* Miguel Cervantes (1547–1616).

l. 20. *he dies, &c. Twelfth Night,* i. v. 261.

l. 21. *Mrs. Siddons.* The actress (1755–1831).

l. 28. *John Hunter.* A famous surgeon (1728–93).

l. 32. *Michaelangelo.* The great painter, sculptor, and architect (1475–1564).

l. 35. *Sir Humphry Davy.* A famous scientist (1778–1829), to whose researches and invention of the Davy safety-lamp countless miners have owed their lives.

P. 59, l. 8. *'A great scholar's memory',* &c. Cf. *Hamlet,* iii. ii. 141.

l. 28. *Molière.* See note to p. 58, l. 11.

Rabelais, The French writer (1495–1552), author of *Gargantua* and *Pantagruel.*

Montaigne. See Introduction.

quote it. Hazlitt himself—to judge by the style—was the author of the obituary notice in the *Examiner.*

P. 60, l. 4. *has not left his peer.* Cf. Milton, *Lycidas,* 9.

l. 13. *The Roman poet.* Horace, *Odes,* iii. i. 40.

l. 17. *'in the instant.' Macbeth,* i. v. 59.

l. 18. *'domestic treason,' &c. Macbeth,* iii. ii. 25.

l. 21. *making it.* Gaining the point, making good the stroke.

l. 23. *the chase.* Corresponding to what in lawn tennis would be called a rally, and what in fives used to be called the 'bully'. (For this and other notes on fives the editor is indebted to Mr. N. J. Chignell, Charterhouse.)

P. 61, l. 14. *Brougham's.* Henry Brougham, afterwards Lord Brougham (1778–1868); Lord Chancellor, writer, and Whig politician.

l. 14. *Canning's.* George Canning (1770–1827), Foreign Minister during the Napoleonic wars. As a bitter opponent of the French Revolution he would not commend himself to the revolutionary Hazlitt.

l. 15. *the Quarterly.* The *Quarterly Review,* a Tory magazine. Hazlitt, as well as Leigh Hunt and Charles Lamb, were among the writers it attacked during the editorship of William Gifford; and an article on *Endymion* was at one time supposed to have been Keats's death-blow.

l. 15. *let ball.* If a played ball strikes an opponent, or an opponent impedes the stroke or the flight of the ball, it is called a 'let', and no account is taken of it.

l. 16. *Cobbett.* William Cobbett (1766–1835), farmer's boy, soldier, political and social pamphleteer. His best-known work is *Rural Rides.*

Junius. The anonymous author, whose identity has never been positively established, of letters in the *Public Advertiser* (1768–73) attacking the Government.

l. 18. *was fourteen.* Had scored fourteen of the fifteen points required to win a game.

l. 38. *Rosemary Branch.* A pleasure resort.

P. 62, l. 19. *with my clenched fist.* Instead of striking the ball with the palm of the hand in the usual way.

l. 20. *Copenhagen House.* A pleasure resort, on the site of which now stands the Caledonian Cattle Market.

l. 25. *Goldsmith consoled himself.* The facts seem to be as follows.—On an occasion when the beauty of some ladies was attracting general attention, Goldsmith uttered the remark, 'There are places where I also am admired'. Hazlitt here—very irrelevantly—introduces a misrepresentation of the incident, to which Boswell's *Johnson* (under date 1763) had given currency.

l. 28. *Mr. Powell.* The proprietor. See below, p. 63, l. 26.

l. 36. *Castlereagh's.* Lord Castlereagh (1769–1822) was Foreign Minister during the Napoleonic wars.

l. 37. *Croker's.* John Wilson Croker (1780–1857), Secretary to the Admiralty; a writer to the *Quarterly Review*; prototype of the venal politician Rigby in Disraeli's *Coningsby.*

P. 63, l. 2. *Mr. Murray.* John Murray (1778–1843), the founder of the publishing house.

l. 25. *In the Fleet, &c.* The Fleet and the King's Bench were debtor's prisons. The liberty allowed to prisoners included the playing of games, and rackets and fives were very popular among them. It is not clear why Hazlitt assumes it would have been in one of these prisons that Cavanagh would have played against Powell, who (see p. 62 l. 28, and below, l. 26) was connected with the Fives-Court in St. Martin's Lane.

l. 26. *open-ground player.* I am unable to conjecture the meaning of this phrase.

l. 28. *we might recommend, &c.* Cf. p. 60, ll. 13–21.

l. 30. *And the best of it is, &c.* I cannot follow the train of argument.

l. 37. *Mr. Peel.* Afterwards Sir Robert Peel.

P. 64, ll. 5–6. *Let no rude hand, &c.* Wordsworth, *Ellen Irwin.*

l. 6. '*Hic jacet.*' 'Here lies.'

THOMAS DE QUINCEY

THOMAS DE QUINCEY (1785–1859) was born in Manchester. In early childhood he lost his father and a favourite sister. He was educated at Bath Grammar School, and later at Manchester Grammar School where he was not happy. After begging in vain to be withdrawn, he one day left school, and, abandoning a first idea of going up to the Lake District to introduce himself to the poet Wordsworth, he trudged the forty miles to Chester where his mother was living. He was allowed to go for a holiday in Wales, but after rambling about for some months he broke off communication with his family, and made his way to London, to raise a loan on some money he was to inherit when he came of age. The negotiations dragged on, and his resources were exhausted, when an encounter with a friend of the family led to a reconciliation. In 1803 he entered Worcester College, Oxford, but he left without taking his degree. At Oxford he had got into the habit of eating opium, to allay pains which he attributed to the injury done his health by his privations in London. He made the acquaintance of the Lake Poets, and for some time lived near them at Grasmere. While there he married a daughter of a neighbouring farmer. The necessity to provide for a family led him to make a final, and ultimately successful, attempt of 'unwinding the accursed chain' of his drug-taking habit. In 1821 the first portion of the *Confessions of an English Opium Eater* appeared. It had an instant success. In 1830 he moved to Edinburgh, where he lived until his death, and was buried. His essays and other writings fill sixteen volumes, and range over an immense field of literature, history, and philosophy, ancient and modern. His fame rests mainly on the *Confessions.* A friend of his quoted the description of a poet in Thomson's *Castle of Indolence* as exactly fitting him—

> A little Druid wight,
> Of withered aspect; but his eye was keen,
> With sweetness mixed. In russet brown bedight
> He crept along, unpromising of mien.
> Gross he who judges so. His soul was fair.

The English Mail Coach (pp. 65–90)

P. 65, l. 7. *Galileo.* The Italian astronomer (1564–1642). It was the satellites of Saturn he discovered.

l. 8. *which is the same thing.* De Quincey in a note adds —'Thus, in the Calendar of the Church festivals, the discovery of the true cross (by Helen, the mother of Constantine) [in A.D. 326] is recorded (and one might think— with the express consciousness of sarcasm) as the Invention of the Cross.'

P. 66, l. 7. *apocalyptic vials.* Bowls containing the wrath of God which the angels are told to pour out. Revelation xv. 7.

P. 68, l. 31. *'snobs.'* The word, at the time De Quincey wrote this essay, meant the rabble.

P. 69, l. 6. *incommunicable.* Unable to be shared (with the inside passengers).

P. 70, l. 24. *jury-reins.* Makeshift reins.

P. 71, l. 12. *Aristotle's.* The moral philosophy of Aristotle (384–22 B.C.) is contained in his *Nicomachean Ethics.*

Zeno's. Zeno (358–260 B.C.) founded the Stoic philosophy.

Cicero's. The philosophy of Cicero, the Roman statesman and orator (106–45 B.C.), is contained chiefly in his work *De Officiis.*

l. 35. *bills.* Bills of exchange, promising to pay a sum at a certain date.

l. 36. *Notes and protestors.* To 'note' or 'protest' a bill of exchange is to make a formal declaration that it has not been paid when due.

l. 38. *house of life.* For the casting of a horoscope the sky is divided into twelve sections called 'houses'.

P. 72, l. 14. *Von Troil's Iceland.* A Swede called Von Troil wrote *Letters on Iceland* (1777), but it is a book by a

Dane called Horrebow, *Natural History of Iceland*, which has one chapter, headed 'Snakes', consisting of the simple sentence—'There are no snakes at all in the island'.

l. 24. *laesa majestas.* Lese-majesty, treason.

ll. 35–6. *jam proximus ardet Ucalegon.* 'Now next Ucalegon begins to blaze.' (II. 311–12).

P. 73, l. 25. *crane-neck quarterings.* 'quarter'=to drive to the side of the road. 'crane-neck'=waggon. (A crane-neck is strictly an iron bar, bent like a crane's neck, which joins the front and back part of a carriage.)

P. 74, l. 9. *potential.* Potent, influential.

l. 22. *echoes of Marengo.* During the battle of Marengo (1800) Napoleon was said to have used these words on hearing of the death of one of his generals.

P. 75, l. 9. *false, fleeting, perjured. Richard III,* I. iv. 55.

l. 12. *Luxor.* A village on the site of the ruins of an ancient Egyptian city.

l. 29. '*which they upon the adverse fashion wanted.*' *Richard III,* v. iii. 12–13.

l. 38. *my heart burn within me.* Luke xxiv. 32.

P. 76, l. 12. *one of our older dramatists.* Thomas Heywood (d. 1650). *Royal King and Loyal Subject.*

l. 14. *omrahs.* Noblemen.

l. 38. *6th of Edward Longshanks, chap. 18.* Longshanks =Edward I. A statute is cited by its own number ('chapter') and the number of the parliament of the sovereign in whose reign it was passed.

P. 77, l. 18. *Non magna loquimur*' but '*vivimus*'. 'We do not talk big' but 'we live big'.

P. 79, l. 21. *Ulysses.* When on his return from Troy he slew Penelope's suitors.

P. 80, l. 7. *Say, all our praises, &c.* 'But all our praises why should lords engross?' Pope, *Moral Essays,* iii. 249.

l. 26. *turrets.* The metalled eyes on the collar through which the reins go.

P. 81. l. 8. '*Perish the roses,' &c.* Wordsworth, *Excursion,* vii. 989.

l. 15. *Mr. Waterton. Wanderings in South America* (1825), Third Journey, ch. iv.

P. 83, l. 36. *attelage.* Coach and horses. (Strictly, a team.)

P. 86, l. 7. *be thou whole.* Luke viii. 48.

P. 87, l. 34. *Gazette.* Official news from the *London Gazette.*

JAMES HENRY LEIGH HUNT

LEIGH HUNT was born in 1784. He was educated, like Charles Lamb, at Christ's Hospital. In 1808, during his editorship of the *Examiner,* he was sentenced to two years' imprisonment for making reflections on the Prince Regent. While in jail he was visited by many sympathizers, including Lamb and Byron. He continued to edit the *Examiner,* in which, in 1816, he introduced Shelley and Keats to the public. He was savagely attacked by the *Quarterly* and *Blackwood's Magazine.* In 1822, with his wife and children, he went out to Italy to join Byron and edit the *Liberal.* He returned to England in 1825. In 1847 he was given a pension. He died in 1859. His writings included poems, essays, dramatic criticisms, and an autobiography. His character is sketched above (Hazlitt, 'The Indian Jugglers', p. 56).

On Getting Up on Cold Mornings (pp. 91–4)

P. 91, l. 1. *Giulio Cordara.* 1704–85.

P. 92, l. 11. *says Milton. Paradise Lost,* II. 295.

P. 93, l. 8. *Queen of France.* Eleanor, wife of Louis VII, who afterwards married Henry II of England.

l. 10. *Emperor Julian.* 'The Apostate', Roman Emperor in the fourth century A.D.

l. 13. *Cardinal Bembo's.* An Italian historian and poet (1470–1547).

Michaelangelo's. See note to p. 58, l. 32.

l. 14. *Titian's.* The Italian painter (1477–1576).

Fletcher's. John Fletcher, the dramatist (1579–1625).

l. 17. *Haroun al Raschid.* Caliph of Baghdad (786–809)— a great prince, and a friend of Charlemagne, but remembered chiefly in connexion with the *Arabian Nights.*

l. 18. *Bedreddin Hassan.* In the tale of Noureddin Ali and Bedreddin Hassan in the *Arabian Nights.*

l. 19. *his mother.* Lady Mary Wortley Montagu (1689–1762).

l. 27. *Sweetly recommends itself, &c. Macbeth*, I. vi. 2.

l. 33. *Thomson.* James Thomson (1700–48).
Seasons. 'Summer', 67.

P. 94, l. 18. *Holborn.* But Holborn is not by any means the longest street in London, nor was it in Leigh Hunt's time.

WALTER BAGEHOT

WALTER BAGEHOT (1826–77) was educated at University College, London, where he distinguished himself in philosophy and political economy. He entered his father's shipowning and banking business; contributed essays to the magazines; became editor of the *National Review*, and later of the *Economist*; and wrote books on political and economic questions, of which the best-known is *The English Constitution.*

Boscastle (pp. 95–101)

P. 95, l. 1. *Mr. Darwin.* 'Boscastle' appeared in the *Spectator* in 1866. The *Origin of Species* had been published seven years before.

P. 96. l. 2. *your most learned contributor.* A reference to the writer of an article on 'The West Country before the Romans', which had appeared in the *Spectator* a short time before.

P. 97, l. 25. *Temple Bar.* This gate, which separated the Strand from Fleet Street, was removed in 1878.

l. 31. *Lilliput.* The country in Swift's *Gulliver's Travels* where the inhabitants were six inches high.

P. 98, l. 4. *Lloyd's.* An association of underwriters for insuring ships and merchandise—called after an Edward Lloyd, who kept a coffee-house in the City where shipowners, underwriters, etc. congregated.

l. 13. *There was no use in going, &c.* i.e. the economic conditions which later were to cause Lombard Street to become the banking centre of London did not at that period exist. (The street was so called after the merchants from Lombardy who settled there in the reign of Henry II.)

l. 35. *Ellangowan.* The home of the Bertrams in Scott's *Guy Mannering.*

l. 36. *'pinners'.* Head-dresses with flaps which were pinned across the breast.

P. 99, 1. 14. '*near Bedford.*' About the time that this essay was published flint implements of the New Stone Age had been found in Bedfordshire.

1. 38. *our Raleighs, &c.* Raleigh and Drake were Devon men, as was Hawkins. Frobisher was born in Yorkshire; Lord Howard of Effingham in Surrey.

P. 100, 1. 11. *Mr. Arnold.* Matthew Arnold's essay *On the Study of Celtic Literature.*

1. 21. *Mr. Kingsley.* Charles Kingsley was born in Devon, but at Holne, not Clovelly.

1. 29. *unsoundness.* It is not clear in what way Bagehot regards Charles Kingsley as 'unsound'.

1. 31. *pure Goth.* Later researches have shown that there is no such thing as a pure Goth or a pure Celt. For at least a thousand years the races have so intermingled that the most that can be said of any individual is that he has a preponderating strain of a certain stock. (Bagehot seems to use 'Goth' as equivalent to 'Teuton', a term which includes many other races besides the Goths proper, who never came to England.)

P. 101, 1. 4. *pragmaticalness.* The dictionary gives, for 'pragmatical', 'meddlesome', 'dogmatic', The alternative suggestion of Bagehot, introduced by 'or', does not seem logically to exclude his first one.

ROBERT LOUIS STEVENSON

STEVENSON was born in Edinburgh in 1850. He was the son of Thomas Stevenson. Father, uncle, and grandfather were lighthouse engineers. He was educated at Edinburgh University, but successively abandoned engineering for law, and law for literature. On account of bad health he spent much of his time abroad in Switzerland and France. In 1880 he married Mrs. Osbourne. He contributed essays to the magazines; collaborated with W. E. Henley in a volume of plays; published *Treasure Island*; and in 1866 established his reputation with the *Strange Case of Dr. Jekyll and Mr. Hyde* and *Kidnapped.* In 1887 he went to America, and settled in the South Sea Islands, at Samoa, where he temporarily recovered health. He died suddenly in 1894. He left a fragment of a posthumous novel, *Weir of Hermiston*, which some regard as his best work.

Walking Tours (pp. 102–9)

P. 102, l. 23. *brown john.* A 'brown george' is an earthenware vessel; a 'demijohn' is a bulging narrow-necked bottle, usually cased in wicker. Stevenson seems to have combined the terms.

P. 103, l. 15. *says Hazlitt.* In 'On going a Journey'.
l. 29. *like Christian.* When, in the *Pilgrim's Progress*, the load fell off his back.
l. 38. *the merchant Abudah.* 'The merchant Abudah was haunted every night by an old hag from whom he only got free by learning to fear God and keep his commandments. See Ridley's *Tales of the Genii*.' (Note by C. B. Wheeler.)

P. 106, l. 13. *make as many articles.* See p. 104, l. 18.

P. 107, l. 13. '*Though ye take,*' &c. From *Areopagitica*.

P. 108, l. 1. *the New Heloïse.* Rousseau's romance, *La Nouvelle Héloise* (1761).
l. 7. *Heine's songs.* Heinrich Heine, the German poet (1799–1856).
Tristram Shandy. By Laurence Sterne (1713–68).
l. 28. '*happy thinking.*' From 'The Rigs of Barley'.

P. 109, l. 17. *You are in the very humour of all social heresy.* You are in a mood to hold views radically opposed to those of orthodox society.

HILAIRE BELLOC

HILAIRE BELLOC, born in 1870, was educated at the Oratory School, Birmingham, and at Balliol College, Oxford. Between leaving school and going to the University he served in the French Artillery. He was Liberal M.P. for Salford 1906–10. His works include poetry, essays, biography, history, travel.

The Little River (pp. 110–13

P. 110, l. 14. *a little river.* The Adur, in Sussex, which runs, about twenty miles, from near Slinfold to New Shoreham.

P. 111, l. 37. *Knight Templar.* A religious military order for the protection of pilgrims to the Holy Land, suppressed in 1312.

GILBERT KEITH CHESTERTON

G. K. CHESTERTON, born in 1874, was educated at St. Paul's School, and attended classes at the Slade School. He is a journalist, critic, essayist, poet.

On Lying in Bed (pp. 114–17)

P. 114, l. 6. *Aspinall.* Aspinall's enamel.

l. 20. *Cyrano de Bergerac.* In the play of that name, by Edmond Rostand (1868–1920). ' I must have some giants'.

l. 34. ' *Use not vain repetitions,*' &c. Matthew, vi. 7.

P. 115, l. 4. *Macedonian Massacres.* A reference to the violent measures with which, during the latter part of the nineteenth century, the Turks were wont to suppress the periodical risings of the inhabitants of Macedonia.

l. 21. *debarred from political rights.* This was written before women were given the vote.

P. 116, l. 10. *Ibsenite pessimists.* i.e. persons like some of the characters in the plays of Henrik Ibsen, the Norwegian dramatist (1828–1906).

l. 28. *Michelangelo.* See note to p. 58, l. 32.

ROBERT LYND

ROBERT LYND, born in Belfast in 1879, is the Literary Editor of the *News Chronicle,* and a regular contributor to the *New Statesman.*

On Good Resolutions (pp. 118–22)

P. 118, l. 25. *Amiel.* Henri-Frédéric Amiel (1821–81), a Swiss professor, known by his *Journal Intime.*

P. 119, l. 23. *Blücher.* The commander of the Prussian army at the battle of Waterloo.

P. 121, l. 21. *Poe quotes.* 'Who knoweth the mysteries of the will? Quoted by Poe, in 'Ligeia' (from Joseph Glanvill: 1636–80).

l. 33. *baffled to fight better.* Robert Browning, ' Epilogue' to *Asolando,* l. 14.

P. 122, l. 15. *the white flower* &c. A reference to Tennyson's Dedication to the Prince Consort of *Idylls of the King,* l. 25—'Wearing the white flower of a blameless life'.

PHILIP EDWARD THOMAS

EDWARD THOMAS, born in 1878, was of Welsh parentage on both sides. He was educated at St. Paul's School and Lincoln College, Oxford. After leaving Oxford he refused several more remunerative openings in order to devote himself to writing. He married early, and had a hard struggle to support himself and his family on the meagre earnings provided by journalism and literature to a writer who during his lifetime was never widely known. He published several volumes of essays; some books on the English countryside (over which he continually rambled); and some historical and literary biographies, including a life of Richard Jefferies. In 1914, influenced by his friend Robert Frost, the American poet, he began to write verse. Shortly after the outbreak of war he enlisted in the Artists Rifles, and was transferred, with a commission, to the Artillery. Freed, for the first time in his life, from the necessity of seeking work from publishers, he continued, in his spare time, the writing of poetry. His first book of poems was published in 1917, a few weeks before he was killed at Arras. A second volume of poems appeared posthumously. Since his death his reputation has gradually grown. Mr. Walter de la Mare writes of him—'When Edward Thomas was killed, a mirror of England was shattered.'

Rain (pp. 123–31)

P. 123, l. 3. *Lear.* See III. ii, iii.

l. 4. *Milton. Il Penseroso*, 130.

l. 7. *Danae's.* Danae was the mother of Perseus by Zeus, who visited her in a shower of gold.

l. 34. *Circean.* Circe was the enchantress who dwelt in the isle upon which Ulysses was cast.

Grieg. The Norwegian composer (1843–1907).

P. 124, l. 16. *Pheidias.* The greatest Greek sculptor (490–432 B.C.). His colossal figure of Zeus, in gold and ivory, was at Olympia.

P. 125, l. 16. '*some natural tears.*' Milton, *Paradise Lost*, 625.

P. 126, l. 11. *lustihead.* Vigour.

l. 24–9. *High trolollie, &c.* From 'Coridon's Song', by J. Chalkhill (*c.* 1600).

P. 127, ll. 7–8. *Tuis hic omnia, &c.* 'Here all is full of thy bounty' (Virgil, *Georgics,* ii. 4–5).

l. 11. *Edmund.* In *King Lear.*

l. 22. *'in his days of nature.'* *Hamlet,* i. v. 12.

l. 25. '*Howl, howl,'* &c. *King Lear,* v. iii. 258.

l. 34. *they.* The houses.

P. 128, l. 39. ' *I know the secret',* &c. Quotation untraced.

P. 129, l. 5. *Blakesmoor.* A house where Lamb in his childhood spent many happy hours, and which he describes in his essay 'Blakesmoor in H——shire'.

l. 12. '*Didone Abandonnata.*' A violin sonata by Tartini (1692–1770).

l. 29. *Sylvans.* Wood-nymphs.

ll. 32–3. *Be present aye, &c.* Virgil, *Aeneid,* vi. 258.

P. 130, l. 15. *Now mark me, &c.* *Richard II,* iv. i. 203, 214.

l. 21. *Car il en est toujours, &c.* There is no question of the literal translation of the phrase—' For there are always some that one can love'; but the application to the context is not clear.

l. 35. *only, we did not know.* That if they had become intimate, the mystery of the house would have vanished.

P. 131, l. 6. '*strange fetters,'* &c. Quotation untraced.

MAX BEERBOHM

MAX BEERBOHM was born in London in 1872. He was educated at Charterhouse and Merton College, Oxford. His books consist of four volumes of essays (*The Works of Max Beerbohm, More, Yet Again, And Even Now*); a book of parodies (*A Christmas Garland*); three works of fiction (*The Happy Hypocrite, Zuleika Dobson,* and the *Dreadful Dragon of Hay Hill*). He is almost equally known for his caricatures, of which he has published six portfolios.

On Going Back to School (pp. 132–5)

P. 132, l. 29. *Vice-Versa.* A story bearing on life at a Preparatory School, by 'F. Anstey' (T. A. Guthrie), 1882.

P. 134, l. 3. *Dabit deus his quoque finem.* 'God will give these too an end'.

P. 135, l. 3. '*damned good-natured friend.*' Sheridan, *The Critic,* i. i.

l. 4. *Romeike.* A press-cutting firm (which supplies authors with reviews of their books).